THE ULTIMATE HISTORY
APTITUDE TEST GUIDE

Published by *RAR Medical Services Limited*
www.uniadmissions.co.uk
info@uniadmissions.co.uk
Tel: +44 (0) 208 068 0438

This book is neither created nor endorsed by the Oxford Faculty of History. The authors and publisher are not affiliated with Cambridge Assessment. The information offered in this book is purely advisory and any advice given should be taken within this context. As such, the publishers and authors accept no liability whatsoever for the outcome of any applicant's History Aptitude Test (HAT) performance, the outcome of any university applications or for any other loss. Although every precaution has been taken in the preparation of this book, the publisher and author assume no responsibility for errors or omissions of any kind. Neither is any liability assumed for damages resulting from the use of information contained herein. This does not affect your statutory rights.

This book contains passages which deal with racism, sexism, and gender identity, among other controversial topics.

About the author

Toby is a professional admissions tutor and has specialised in the HAT since the completion of his DPhil in History at Green Templeton College, Oxford. He has been teaching for over ten years, both as admissions coach and as a course-coordinator for History at Christ Church, Oxford. In that time he has also worked as a manuscript examiner for the HAT and as a civilian consultant to the NASA Ames Research Centre's Human Factors division in California.

THE ULTIMATE HAT GUIDE

TECHNIQUES AND PRACTICE QUESTIONS

Toby Bowman

Rohan Agarwal

UniAdmissions

CONTENTS

INTRODUCTION: WHAT THIS BOOK IS FOR

Fundamentally, there is a lot more to the HAT than meets the eye. It is, at first appearance, a single question, which requires a single answer and it is easily written off by teachers as an easy exam or worse, one which cannot be prepared for.

If you are reading this, then you know this isn't the case.

The HAT may be a single question, but the outcome of the test can have a profound impact on your chances of admission. It's important that you *get it right*. The problem is that there hasn't been a way to get to grips with which skills you need to develop, and the ways in which you should develop them, until now!

In this book, we are going to give you all the tools you need to understand the questions in the HAT, analyse their sources, and deliver brilliant answers. There are a whole host of different techniques involved in a truly good HAT answer.

WHY THE HAT?

We will begin with an overview of the HAT itself, why it was developed and how it works. One of the most important things for any applicant, when they approach an exam, is to have an understanding of what the exam's purpose is, what they are expected to demonstrate. This first section will walk you through the reasoning behind the HAT's creation, with input from actual HAT examiners. When you approach the rest of the core content and our practice tests, you'll be able to picture just what you are meant to do, what *every* candidate is meant to do. If you can do it, you're on your way to getting a top mark in the HAT.

HOW IS THE HAT USED?

We will also walk you through the decision-making process made by examiners when they are considering HAT results, how heavily is it weighted, how do different results affect the outcomes? We will focus, obviously, on what happens if you do well. You have the guide, after all! This section will also walk you through the variety of different ways that the HAT can influence the questions you are asked at interview. Candidates often don't realise that *everything* they submit to the university is fair game for the interview process, including test manuscripts, and their answer can either help them or hinder them when they get invited to interview (which you hopefully will). For more practice interview questions, you can also check out our Ultimate Oxbridge Interview Guide. Here in the Ultimate HAT Guide, we will talk about some of the ways in which your response can guide the interview so that you can make use of that in your interview preparation, you have an area to practice and anticipate.

WHAT IS THE HAT EXPERIENCE?

One of the most important aspects of exam preparation, and one which is also one of the hardest to prepare candidates for, is the experience of sitting the exam. Schools do a fairly good job with mock exams, but the HAT, like every other exam, is subtly different. What we will do here is walk you through where you will have to go, the way that the test centre will look, what you'll have to do, and generally what your experience of the HAT process itself should be like. We have sections here for people sitting the HAT in the UK and Overseas, so you're covered regardless. We will also, here, give you valuable information for how to handle other candidates sitting the exam with you, and our tips might just make the crucial difference in helping you remain calm and focused in the run-up to and participation in your test.

HAT BASICS - QUESTIONS

The next phase is more technical. Here, we will provide all the techniques, tips, and information required to pull all the information you can out of the questions themselves. HAT questions are written in a specific way, and if you can learn what the hidden language of HAT questions is, then you are on your way to having a step-by-step guide to what you need to write about, right in front of you in the test. Hopefully, the importance of this is obvious, but we will walk you through the various stages of processing, deconstructing, and reorganising questions so that you can make the very most of them. This is also really useful, more broadly, for people taking a range of tests with essay questions. If you ever struggle to work out what you can talk about in an answer, and what isn't relevant, this section will really help you beyond the confines of the HAT, as well as in it.

In this section we will also cover some of the other fundamentals of technique for the HAT. The first is how to use the information you have learned from the question to inform your reading of the HAT extract. Once you're finished with the guide, you should have all the information required to put together a 'filter' for the exam text, which will allow you to highlight and pull together all of the fragments of the passage that will help you answer your question in a single sweep. This can save you a huge amount of time, and also reduce the risk of those pesky 'low-level indicator' warnings that countless examiners see where a candidate has misunderstood, misused, or plain misquoted part of the text. That's never good.

The last part we will deal with in this section is about defining terms. This is a pet peeve of many examiners, where there is a specific term in the question (let's use, for an example, something particularly nasty like 'cultural') which goes critically unaddressed by the candidate. We will walk you through how to go about identifying which terms require definitions, how to create your own, how to defend them, and how to use them. We will also cover how to maximise the value of your definitions so that you can reasonably write the answer you can give best without appearing to miss out on otherwise necessary talking points. In this section, we will also have a handful of example questions, terms, and definitions from HAT style questions to show you how best to do this.

HAT BASICS – EXTRACTS

This section is larger than the last, and really that shouldn't be surprising. By far the largest single component of the HAT is the extract, often several pages of text. In the HAT Basics – Extracts section of The Ultimate HAT Guide, we'll give you a detailed rundown of what you want to do, as well as all the techniques you need to work out what the central themes of the extract are. This is important because once you have understood what the question wants you to talk about, identifying the author's main aim, their purpose, is crucial to understanding how the question relates to the extract, and this can drastically shape your answer. Don't worry, we will show you how.

We'll show you how to identify the main points in the question, and relate each one to a theme of the extract, and build a really clear understanding of why the examiner's picked it. You should reach a point where you can read the question, look at the extract, and be able to say to yourself 'I know why they picked this one'.

It's also in this section that you'll find our guide to reading extracts. Now you might be thinking, while you read this introduction, that you're clearly capable of reading, and you are! We aren't out to insult your intelligence. Reading extracts is best approached in a specific way though, and we will give you a guide to how best to read (and, if necessary, re-read) the passage in order to not only understand what it says but understand what goes unsaid.

HAT ULTIMATE TACTICS – SOURCE ANALYSIS

You should, by this point, have been given good coverage of the basics, how to understand the question, how to use that to read and understand the extract, and this can set you up for planning out an answer. It isn't enough to just be able to comprehend the material. In Ultimate Tactics, we'll give you a detailed walkthrough of the fundamental skills which are *absolutely required* to be able to do well in the HAT.

The first thing is source analysis. Source analysis skills are vital to any historian, and you will already have been taught many of the fundamentals of this by teachers (at least, hopefully). The HAT is testing the best history applicants in the world though, and so they expect candidates to all have advanced source analysis skills more commonly found in history students at Oxford. What we will do is give you a complete, detailed guide to source analysis, with examples that we will go through together, so that you can understand what to do and how. In this section, we will also cover the basics (don't worry) but this will all be oriented specifically to the kinds of sources you are given in the HAT. We'll not only talk about how to draw all the information possible from sources, but also how to learn from what the source is, and it's very existence. We'll provide breakdowns for all of the major source types seen in HAT questions, as well as the tools for developing your own (on the off chance that they give you a source type never seen in the HAT before). Anything can happen in the HAT, and it is incredibly important to have your own set of solid source analysis skills so that no matter what the exam paper looks like, you can write a top-tier answer.

We'll also have work in here on limitations, how to determine what the *problems* are in the extracts they give you. HAT exam writers love to set complex questions on unusual extracts, which will *always* have at least one glaring flaw. They are often easy to spot, but the very best candidates are able to show how they are working with those limitations, compensating for them, or even using them to their advantage. We will show you how to do this. We'll also give a detailed guide of how to deal with the sticky issue of authorship, this one trips up candidates the most out of any source analysis issues, and we'll cover how to analyse the Author's world, and learn from their assumptions in a way that is concrete and applicable to your exam results.

The last section of the Source Analysis section of Ultimate Tactics focuses on you. As the person sitting the exam, the way you relate to the extract you're reading is incredibly important. It is vital that you learn how to recognise your own biases and worldviews. This will include helping you put yourself in the shoes of a contemporary reader, and suspending your disbelief in appraising sources. This is so important because one of the major pitfalls candidates stray into is discounting information in a source which they know to be wrong, or fanciful (there was one year where the extract contained a detailed description of people living in Scandinavia with dog's heads. It did not go well). There is a lot of material you'll be exposed to in extracts which won't, at first glance, make sense or will seem to be a flight of fancy by the author. We will give you the tools needed to work out what useful points you can draw from seemingly 'meaningless' information.

HAT ULTIMATE TACTICS – ESSAY PLANNING

Source analysis alone will give you the means to really efficiently extract valuable information from the extract given to you in your HAT paper. That won't help you much when you come to writing your answer. This is a really important stage in any essay-based exam, and the tips we give you here will be valuable across a wide range of topics, but these are tuned specifically for the HAT. You have a very limited amount of time, and a *lot* of information to process. It is important that you have refined your essay writing process as much as possible.

We'll give you a number of key tactics for approaching your essays, starting with planning. To a lot of us, essay planning can feel like a pointless chore which sucks up time you could otherwise spend writing the perfectly good plan in your head. We'll show you why this isn't quite the case, and how a good plan can drastically improve your chances of excelling in the HAT.

In this guide we will not only walk you through the methodology behind a good plan, and how to make the best use of essay plans in the HAT, but we'll also give you a step-by-step guide to take the examiner's requirements from the question, and the central themes of the extract you have already learned to identify, and turn those into a detailed, efficient plan of attack for your writing so that when your pen hits the paper, it doesn't have to stop again until you've finished. As a part of this, we will also give you some top tips on how to establish and maintain narrative flow. Your essay doesn't just have to be efficient and on-topic, it has to make sense. Planning is the stage in which you ensure that each of your points flow together and form a single thread which examiners can make sense of. If they can understand what you are saying, they can more easily give you marks.

HAT ULTIMATE TACTICS – WRITE

Your source analysis, question dissection, reading skills, planning, have all come together. At some point, you actually have to write your answer. A lot of students have failed long before they have reached this point. However, with the Ultimate HAT Guide, this hopefully won't happen to you. You have got to make sure that you can carry your brilliant appraisal of the question through to an equally brilliant final manuscript, and your writing skills are crucial to that. We have collected tips from HAT examiners, essay writers, and teachers and distilled them into what we think are the most important techniques for essay writing, our Ultimate Tactics.

Here we'll walk you through how to make sure all of your points are well supported, how to make sure your evidence is suitable for a HAT answer, and how to properly use quotations in your responses. We'll help you develop the skills required to avoid repeating yourself, to write analytically rather than descriptively, and to ensure that your analysis is conducted in a way which can be clearly tied to what the examiner wants you to talk about. We'll also have some tips in here on good English, and a timing guide for reading, planning, and writing in the HAT (though this will be influenced to a certain extent by your personal reading and writing speeds).

HAT ULTIMATE TACTICS – THE MARK SCHEME

There are many HAT tests online with mark schemes that students can work on. The problem they all have is that the mark scheme follows a number of internal rules which are either poorly explained or not explained at all. We will give you a detailed breakdown of how the HAT mark scheme works, and how you can make sure that your answer fulfils the criteria for a top tier answer. We'll go through just what a 'top tier answer' really is, what it looks like, and how you can deliver one. We will also talk about the ways in which examiners decide whether an essay really is top tier or not so that you can practice making the most of your answer. You want it to be clearly, and obviously, of the highest level to the examiner as they read it, and with our help, you should have a good chance of doing so.

We'll also bring in some tips from former HAT examiners, and a breakdown of what they want you to do. We asked them what a perfect HAT candidate would write, they told us, we've put it in this book for you. If you can do that, you may well be on your way to HAT success.

WHAT'S NEXT?

This book gives you the tools needed to become a HAT ace. The last section of this book provides a number of tests you won't have seen before, all in the style of the HAT, for you to practice on. We will also talk you through what you can expect after you have finished your HAT, and wish you good luck.

As for right now, while you read this, the rest of the guide is ahead. In it should be all the information you need to get a fantastic mark in the HAT and pave your way to becoming an Oxford historian. Don't feel like you have to do it all at once, however, we'd recommend you start at the beginning.

Good luck!

WHY HISTORY?

If you're contemplating the HAT, then obviously you're also considering reading history. Although this won't come up in the HAT, it is quite common for them to use the HAT passage, and question, to encourage you to answer the question 'why is history important?'

In other words, it might be helpful to examine why we study history at all, and why you might want to.

We aren't going to go into great detail on the cultural and human benefits of historical investigation, but over the next couple of pages, we are going to look at why people choose to study history, and why you might want to as well. The majority of successful candidates for history subjects at Oxford will have a decent understanding of the main principles and skills of history, and will be able to use them and make reference to them in their response to the HAT. This is particularly valuable because it can help you refine your understanding of why HAT examiners work in the way they do, and what they are looking for. It can also be helpful in the rest of your admissions process.

HAT examiners have, on more than one occasion, set questions which have been about the power of history – either through examining the danger historical knowledge can pose (to either the holder of that knowledge or those seeking to suppress it) – or by getting you to demonstrate how the extract you have been given can *transform* understandings of specific concepts.

In order to help you to properly respond to these kinds of questions, which aren't just about something in history but about history itself, we need to start with the notion of dangerous history. One of the many reasons that history books are among those burned, banned or rewritten is because of the relevance their narrative holds to identity. Particularly, in many cases, history is the basis for people's sense of national, racial or cultural identity. Notions of 'who we are' and particularly 'who we are different from' stem from an historical basis. Our past informs our current expectations, preferences and prejudices. Your first thought, then, might be that history actually sounds like a pretty bad idea, if it is used for so much evil. The main issue with that is one of the alternatives. If we remove all the history books and we stop teaching it, we create an environment in which people have no idea how we got to where we are today. A lot of how we got to where we are today (at least in the industrialised world) is quite unpleasant, but in the absence of that knowledge you have a vacuum which can be filled with any information at all. People can lie, create fake stories, and tell you that where we are today isn't so bad, because of something worse that happened before. They can tell you that your people or your country are under threat from an historic enemy. They can tell you that something atrocious never happened, and without history, you can't even begin to challenge them because there would be no reason to. This is the crux of the issue; history is a means to limit misinformation. Its pursuit, especially in a world where information can be created, propagated and consumed at incredible speeds and with greater complexity than ever before, is vital in helping to establish what is and what isn't true.

The issue of 'truth' is a sticky one and, if you decide to apply for history and succeed, you'll do a lot more work on just what is and is not true at that point. We can't, fundamentally, know *everything* about what happened in the past, we can just know about enough of it to point us toward what is more likely to be true than not. Over time, and as we learn, that process becomes more accurate and decisive. As a history applicant, the HAT examiners will want you to be able to demonstrate some of the judgment skills required in this process. The *HAT is not a test of historical knowledge*. It is a test of your historical *process*. You don't need to read up on countless different areas of history, but you do need to know how history works and why people study it. Helping you approach the truth, and recognise outright lies, is one of the main reasons.

Historical knowledge can, and will, be incredibly useful more specifically, in helping you understand the way that countries work, the ways in which humans have coexisted (peacefully or otherwise) in the past, and perhaps even your own environment, among others. The human past is a colossal topic, and no history student can ever really be a generalist. There will be areas that you never even hear of, after decades of study. For some, the endless mystery is part of the appeal, but if you can identify the topics that you like, and find interesting, that is incredibly valuable in your future studies.

In the HAT, though, we need to remain focused on the 'why history' question more broadly. Part of this we have already discussed here. The rest is about transferrable skills. The main job of a history student, and a historian, is to create a better understanding of the past through comprehensive research. Finding new sources of information, critically evaluating them, and combining them into a narrative which makes sense is a core component of history. For the HAT, examiners want you to demonstrate your ability to do exactly that. Specifically, they want you to demonstrate your ability to carefully and intelligently consider a source of information, and from it render a 'judicious interpretation of the past'.

What that means is make clear statements about what life was like in the past, based on what you can learn from the source you have been given, and ensure that each and every one of your observations has a stated line of thinking from your evidence to your statements. This process of source analysis will be, once honed, of considerable value to you both in the course of your degree (no matter what you study) and your life. When you couple that with the research skills that you'll develop as part of your programme of study, you'll be leaving university with a proven ability to synthesise large amounts of highly complex qualitative and quantitative data, and carry out a detailed analysis. Skills like that adorn many job descriptions across a variety of sectors, and if pursuing history as a career ends up not being for you, it will still serve you extremely well.

The last main advantage of pursuing history here, among humanities subjects at least, is its opportunities for interdisciplinary work. History draws together the detailed analytics of an English degree with the research requirements of law and requires a good understanding of human philosophy and ethics. It draws all of those components together into a degree which gives you tangible skills for future life and, more importantly, a really good understanding not only of how the world works but *why*.

If you would like to study a history-based subject, then we'd best get to work on the test itself.

WHAT IS THE HAT?

The History Aptitude Test was introduced in 2004, amidst some criticism from social commentators at the time. The objective was to drastically reduce the number of candidates being invited to interview for History-based degrees at the University of Oxford.

The HAT, from 2018 onwards, comprises a single question taken in the space of **one hour**. The examiners have decided that they only need one question to sufficiently narrow the pool of applicants chosen for interview.

Fundamentally, the HAT will comprise a single passage, followed by a single question. The passage could be from any kind of medium, any time, and any subject, but it will always constitute a primary source. In the HAT, candidates will be expected to show that they know how to read and analyse the source and write about it concisely. In general, candidates are expected to write 2-3 sides of A4 paper, but you're given eight just in case. You shouldn't ever run out of space to write in the HAT, if you do you'll have written too much.

What this means is that the HAT is a test of your reading comprehension skills, a test of your source analysis skills, a test of your critical thinking skills and a test of your writing skills. The HAT is, therefore, also a test of your ability to balance all of those skills, and considering how short it is, also a test of your time management skills. The examiners provide a note in the exam, telling you how they think you should divide your time as a rough guide, and it is something which many applicants still get wrong. In the Timing section of this guide we will give you a detailed breakdown of how you should use your time in the HAT, and you can refine that to suit your personal style through the practice tests.

The source that you will be given will be about two pages long, perhaps longer. These are often chosen for their complexity or unusual nature and will have complex issues surrounding provenance, authorship or purpose. Sadly, we can't say with more certainty what will be in the next test (if only we could) but it will have the following format:

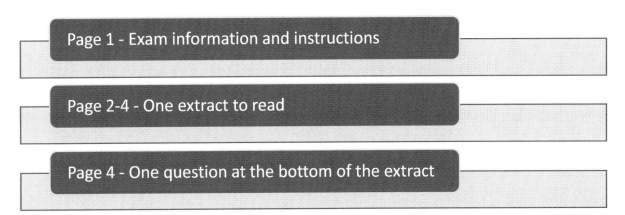

Page 1 - Exam information and instructions

Page 2-4 - One extract to read

Page 4 - One question at the bottom of the extract

The HAT then is a test which is used to decide whether or not you will be interviewed, but it comes down to a single question at the end of a single, quite long piece of text. All you know, at this stage, is that the text will be fairly tricky to understand, and even hard to extract historical information from. In order to understand just how you can make the most of the test, and show your quality, we should take a look at just what the Examiners are looking for, and why they use the HAT in the first place.

WHY DO TUTORS USE THE HAT?

Aptitude tests had once been a staple of selective universities throughout the UK. These were phased out in the 1980s and 1990s, but in the late 90s and early 2000s, the number of applications to university increased. At the same time, applicants were increasingly smart and well educated, and this meant that the average number of 'A' grades at A-Level shot up (you couldn't get A* grades at A level back then). This meant that Oxford admissions tutors were increasingly struggling to work out which AAA candidates they should invite to interview, and which AAA candidates they should reject. One of the most popular subjects to apply for at Oxford was History, and so the problem was particularly pronounced there. As a solution, the HAT was devised as a preliminary filter. The idea was that, by requiring applicants to complete another examination beyond their A-levels, it would be possible to further refine the list of candidates.

For this to be meaningful, however, the test had to be functionally different from the History A-Level, otherwise the people who had performed well at school would, most likely, perform well in the HAT, and it would be meaningless. As a result, the HAT was designed to test a candidate's ability and historical skill, their *aptitude,* rather than their recall skills.

That remains the case today. While the test has undergone some (fairly minor) changes since its introduction 16 years ago, the main aim is to thin the herd, to ensure that only applicants with a high level of historical aptitude *and* great grades *and* a great personal statement get through to the interview phase. What this means, of course, is that we need to make sure that you not only have that level of aptitude but (far more importantly) you are able to *show* it.

TESTING INTELLIGENCE

One of the main purposes of the HAT is to test each candidate's ability to think creatively and intelligently about a source. What that encompasses is thinking about the ways in which history works, and incorporating that into your own attempts to put yourself in the shoes of the person who created the source in the first place, and communicating to the examiner what you can learn about the world they lived in. We will walk you through how to do that in a minute, but what is important to take from this is that the admissions tutors are giving you an opportunity to show your skills as an historian, and you need to make the most of it.

Your ability to hold the worldview of the source's author in your head, alongside your own, is mainly a test of intelligence. If you're sitting the HAT, odds are you're fairly smart as it is, but the admissions tutors will often make creative use of tricky sources to see which candidates are able to forget, temporarily, about what they know about the world around them and place themselves in another time, and another *way of thinking.* You have to show that you can infer and draw conclusions from the things that the author has assumed, or that they know, and use that to make larger statements about specific elements of the world around them like culture, or social values (this will be determined by your specific question).

TESTING ACCURACY

Another reason that admissions tutors devised the HAT, and still use it today, is that it can be an excellent test of a candidate's ability to pay attention to detail and be accurate in their reading *and* their writing.

By providing you with a complex source, and a very broad question, they hope to force candidates into two main groups – those which focus on description, and those which focus on analysis. Analysis is the one you want to go for in the exam, the basic difference is that analysis focuses on what the data in the source can tell you about the factor(s) specified in the question, while description focuses on extracting data from the source which relates to those factors and arranging it in an essay format.

The breadth of the question is deceptive. Questions will normally look something like this:

What can we learn from this passage about the society that the author lived in?

At first, that might seem to be fairly vague, 'society' is an incredibly broad term. So how is this testing your accuracy? In fact, they are looking to see how accurately you can learn from the passage – how much detail can you find in the extract, and just how much *can* you say about society without making any guesses. They are also looking at how accurate you can be in your response to the 'society' issue. Society can refer to a lot of things, and one of the things that admissions tutors use the HAT for is to determine which candidates are able to take control of a broad topic like that, and turn it into something specific. Identify what is and is not society, and show the examiners that you have been able to pick out everything from the extract which addresses the society of the author. That attention to detail and precision isn't something which is particularly assessed by A-Level examinations, at least not to the level that they are going to be scrutinising it here, so your ability to be accurate is important. Moreover, this will really serve you in the subsequent undergraduate study, which is one of the reasons why they want to make sure that all of the candidates they interview are good at it.

TESTING YOUR ABILITY TO RESPOND TO THE UNKNOWN

One of the defining components of regular exams is your ability to prepare through learning a set specification, knowing what content will appear, and then being able to recall that content and use it to score high marks. The HAT was designed to work differently. There is no specification and there is *zero* historical content that you can learn in order to prepare. This was done deliberately so that there was a level playing field of applicants who had all had access to the same amount of prior knowledge, and the test would, therefore, be solely a test of aptitude, rather than memory work.

What this means is that you are not expected to know anything about what is talked about in the primary source you'll be working on. In fact, you will be **heavily penalised** for using knowledge you do have about the subject if you happen to know any. Another reason admissions tutors use the HAT is because it gives them a way to test how well you handle the unknown. You're sat in a test, and you're asked to talk about (for example) the society of 16th century Genoa. You don't know anything about 16th century Genoa (if you do, pretend you don't). Your objective is to write a multiple-page essay on the society of 16th century Genoa with zero prior knowledge, and only one source of information: the extract. It isn't from a textbook, and it isn't going to be didactic. You must respond to the unknown by using your intelligence, and your precision, to determine the full extent of knowledge you can derive from that source, and where you got it from.

If you can do that, then you'll be well on your way to showing the admissions tutors that you have all the skills required to excel in the degree they are assessing you for, and one step closer to an offer, and a place at Oxford.

TESTING COMMUNICATION

This last one is related to the point we made above, about showing where you got your information from. One of the things which admissions tutors are really keen on these days is clarity of expression and good communication of knowledge. This means that you need to make sure that your logic, your thinking, is clearly spelt out and that when you make statements about your logic or your conclusions you can point to a specific piece of evidence you've identified from the extract and say 'and that's why'.

This is, to a certain extent, also tested in your A-Levels, at least those with essay components. The difference here is that you are being asked to draw conclusions about a topic you know nothing about, and that means that all of your claims have to be entirely derived from the extract. You've got to be able to make it easy for the person reading your essay to know why you are saying what you are saying. It also means that sometimes, the conclusions that you draw will be in direct contradiction of either what you know, or common sense. For example, if an extract talks about the fact that women couldn't be suspects in a church robbery because they are incapable of theft, you can make a point about the fact that in the author's society, women were understood to be incapable of theft, even though you know that this was blatantly not the case. The claims which you know are shaky, or don't make sense, but which are clearly what the author believed to be true are some of the ones which are hardest to communicate well. We will cover, in detail, how to go about doing that in the Source Analysis section of HAT Survival Essentials.

THE VALUE OF THE HAT TO ADMISSIONS TUTORS

All of these things are, in one way or another, also tested in your A-Levels, they know that you have a certain level of intelligence, precision, and communication skills in order to be able to get to the point of applying with predicted A* grades. The HAT tests different aspects of these in a combination you don't see otherwise. The reason that it has been in use for so many years is precisely that admissions tutors believe that it will challenge you in a different way to any of your other exams, and so some candidates who have aced their school work might perform terribly in the HAT.

The examiners who mark your HAT will be looking for you to demonstrate all the criteria above. They want you to show that you can creatively and accurately analyse a source to learn a huge amount of information about a specific element of the human past *in a vacuum*. They also want you to communicate it well, the better you can do that the easier it will be for them to read, understand, and mark your work. The final score they generate will be passed on to the admissions tutors considering your application, and they will use that to inform their understandings of your abilities as you compare to *the rest of the people applying to Oxford for a History-based degree*. Unlike your A-Levels, which give you a grade that is standardised across the entire cohort (not just in the UK, thousands take A-Levels each year in other countries), your HAT result is situated within the context of how applicants performed. This means your final mark will put you in a very small band, which joins the rest of your application in consideration for who will, and will not, be invited. We will look at just how that final mark factors into your application next.

HOW DOES THE HAT AFFECT YOUR APPLICATION?

One of the questions that we get asked the most about the HAT is just how much does it have an impact. How important is it *really?* A lot of the answers that you get online are vague, and the reasons for this is that there are a range of different factors which can impact how important the HAT is to your application, and on top of that the HAT itself is one in a range of factors in your application.

What we can do though, is try to spell out the different things which can affect the importance of your HAT result, and therefore the extent to which it impacts your application. Your own personal circumstances as an applicant are of course unique, and so the answer will vary slightly from person to person. This should give you the means to work out just where your HAT might come in handy.

COLLEGE CHOICE
Choosing which college you would like to apply to is, for many Oxford applicants, an important component of their application to university. It isn't the case here, that there are 'good' and 'bad' colleges, for applying to read History or for the HAT. What is true is that each college will have different admissions tutors, and the amount of weight they choose to attach to your HAT grade will be informed by their own sets of rules and values. This is something which, in theory, is standardised, but the reality is different. Don't let your choice of college be changed by this, as there's no way of knowing for sure what impact your choice of college will have. For more on choosing colleges, the Ultimate Guide to Oxbridge Colleges might be valuable.

SUBJECT CHOICE
Applicants taking the HAT are taking one of a number of different courses, all involving history, but which have their own unique identities. For example, if you are applying to read History and Economics, you will also have to take the Thinking Skills Assessment. This can mean that your HAT result becomes one of a larger number of factors which are considered. It doesn't become unimportant, but an exemplary or terrible grade may have a *slightly* diminished impact. In subjects where the HAT is your only aptitude test, it is more important than ever to ensure you get a great final mark.

ACADEMIC PERFORMANCE

Your academic performance outside of the HAT can also have a bearing on how it is weighted by admissions tutors. If you're coming into the HAT with a raft of A* grades at GCSE and predicted at A-Level, they alone won't make much difference, because the majority of other applicants will too, however, achievements beyond your exams, things like essay prize submissions (and wins) can make it clear that you can excel beyond the boundaries of typical school education (which is the same thing the HAT is trying to assess). If you can show that, it means that a poor HAT results *might* count against you a little less, while a great HAT result will show that you have experience with advanced history work and, crucially, that you are consistent which may have a very positive impact on your application.

WRITTEN SUBMISSIONS

Another important part of your application to Oxford for a History subject is your written submissions. While this book doesn't deal with those, if you can submit great written work which, particularly, shows off your source analysis skills and your ability to conduct independent research, it will mean that in your HAT you will have the opportunity to display those same skills again in a setting where you couldn't possibly have outside help. A good HAT score when you have good written submissions can produce more than the sum of the whole because it confirms that your writing and research skills are great (from your written submissions) and are entirely yours (because you duplicate them in the HAT).

WHAT HAPPENS IF YOUR HAT IS VERY GOOD

The average HAT score for candidates *made offers* in 2019 was a little under 70%. If you score above 85% it *does not guarantee that your application will be considered*. It does, however, make it a lot more likely that minor issues or detracting factors in the rest of your application will be overlooked, and it will, therefore, increase your odds of securing an offer. Between 85 and 100%, the difference made to your application is an exercise in diminishing returns, and we generally advise that applicants aim to consistently secure at least 80% to ensure that they get the best chance for their application. The tools and tips in this guide should make that far more likely.

Provided that your HAT score is above 85% or so, which you should all be shooting for, there are still things that can derail your application, a great HAT score is not a panacea. Badly written work or worse, a poor reference, will do a great deal of damage which a good score in the HAT cannot absolve. If they are looking at a glowing HAT transcript in one hand, and a reference saying you're poorly behaved and inattentive in the other... it cannot fix everything. What a great score *does do* is twofold: it gets you through the first stage of the screening process, and it can *mitigate minor issues* with other parts of your application, which are almost inevitable. Somewhere along the line there will probably be a typo you miss in your personal statement or a missed reference in your written work, and a great HAT score can help admissions tutors give you the benefit of the doubt.

... AND WHAT IF IT IS VERY BAD

If your HAT score is around 60% or lower, then it can have a very negative effect on your application. Remember, admissions tutors use the HAT to filter the applicants, all of whom have great academic results on their application. If you don't get a decent score in the HAT, you are being *caught in that first filter*. The average score for people getting offers was around 69% in 2019, and that's generally consistent year on year. If you score outside of five percent below that, you can reasonably expect your application to suffer.

HOW DOES THE HAT INFLUENCE YOUR INTERVIEWS?

If you do well in the HAT, you'll be invited to interview. While interview preparation is not covered in this guide, there are a couple of ways in which your performance in the HAT can influence the interview process, and knowing that means that you can maximise the value of your HAT preparation in ensuring that both the exam and the subsequent interview go as well as possible.

The interview process is inherently amorphous and impossible to accurately predict, however, we've drawn together a collection of interview questions which students have been asked which are based on an aspect of their response to the HAT. We'll walk you through the best way to respond to these questions and, where appropriate, how your approach to the HAT can set you up for success in the interview as well!

Question 1: Why do you think we chose a source based on [the topic in your HAT exam]?

- This one is one of the more common HAT based questions. What they are looking for in the interview is for you to show an understanding of the historical process and the reasoning behind the HAT itself. In your response, you should talk about the fact that they wanted a source which forced students to employ a range of different analytical techniques. When you sit the HAT, try to take a mental note of the particular challenges posed by the source you are reading, what makes it interesting? If you can work out why they chose this one to test you, it will mean that if you're asked that question at interview you can shine.

Question 2: How do you think you might change your response now you've had more time to reflect on it?

- This question is a tricky one. It can make you second guess yourself and retract or change your entire argument in the HAT, because you think there must be something wrong with it to ask this question. Remember, they have invited you to interview afterwards, you have done well in the HAT. Don't offer a retraction, instead talk about how you might expand upon points you already made. The best way to do this is, in your HAT exam, make a mental note of the minor points which you don't have time to reasonably talk more about. That way, in the interview, you can talk about elements of your HAT response that you *could* change, and whether you would or not depends on your personal judgement. Ideally, your original HAT response will be great, but that doesn't mean you can't tweak it slightly. Remember the topics you noted in your exam, but didn't expand on, and focus on those.

Question 3: Here is the context of the source, does that change your interpretation of [an aspect of the exam]

- With this question, the interviewers are going to give you new information and they are primarily testing your ability to respond flexibly to it. The way that you can integrate your HAT preparation into curating your response is by making sure that, when you are practicing source analysis, you always consider what your assumptions are regarding the context of the source. In the source analysis section, we will examine just how to make conclusions about the context of HAT sources, and if you are given that information at interview, you can talk about the way that the source's context affects the way that you would analyse it, and that can also tell you about the conclusions you can make about whatever aspect of the exam they are quizzing you about!

Question 4: Could you tell us a bit more about why you argued [something you said in your HAT exam response]

- A bit like question 2, this one can sometimes trip candidates up and make them think you need to change or retract something. If you are at interview, the odds are that it's because your HAT answer was good, so they won't be wanting you to suggest major changes to your work. Here, they want you to elaborate on your thinking, and explain the link between the source and what you said [they should either tell you what you said, or let you read your response again]. In the HAT, it is very important that you clearly demonstrate these logical links for all of the points you make in response to the question, and if you can do that, it means that this question will only be in response to points you have already done a fairly good job of evidencing, and your discussion can follow what you have already said.

Question 5: What other experience do you have of source analysis? (this can come up if your HAT was very good or bad)

- This question can come up either if your HAT response was superb, or if it was a little sub par. They want you to talk to them about what practice you have done with analysing sources in the past. In your case, you will have practiced with loads of sources in this book, which is a start, but you should try to make sure that you talk about research that you have conducted in your own time or as part of school work on primary material. In terms of HAT preparation, make sure you've done lots of source analysis! Identify what primary sources you have come across in your school work, or in extracurricular study, and apply the techniques in this book to those. That way, you can bring in a range of evidence of your experience beyond 'I read a UniAdmissions book'.

Question 6: Why do you think we made you take the HAT?

- Luckily for you, this question is one which we have already answered above! They want you to show that you've got some awareness of the value of the HAT, and crucially, the importance of good source analysis skills to undergraduate study. The way to integrate your HAT preparation into anticipating this question is to make sure you are familiar with the origins and purpose of the HAT, and that you have a clear understanding of why good source analysis skills matter!

Question 7: If you were given this source again in your undergraduate studies, how would you approach it?

- This question is rarer than the others, as it is often replaced by a broader question about your approach to historical material, but it can be based on the HAT. Here, they want you to demonstrate your ability to devise and talk about a research process - in your undergraduate studies, crucially, you won't be in an exam. Recall how in the HAT you couldn't bring in any of your own knowledge, and talk here about the ways in which you would find knowledge to bring in! Crucially, this requires you to talk about how you would conduct research on the setting of the source, so when you are preparing for the HAT, make sure you pay attention to the section in this book on Nature, Origin, and Purpose, so that you know what the source was from, and can talk about what topics you would research if you were re-evaluating it as an undergraduate student of History at Oxford.

HOW TO SIT THE HAT, AND WHAT IT WILL BE LIKE – UNITED KINGDOM

For the majority of applicants sitting the HAT within the UK, you'll be taking the HAT at your own school. It should be treated by your school like any other exam, so expect to have to sit the exam in silence. Depending on how many of your year are taking the HAT at your school, it might be in a much smaller venue that most of your other exams though.

Oxford has few requirements for candidates sitting the exam, though you aren't allowed to bring in any books or notes, and you must write in black pen only. You are allowed to bring in pens, pencils, erasers, highlighter pens, clear pencil cases, any medicine you are taking, tissues and a clear plastic water bottle (provided that you remove the label before you go in.) You will also need to provide some form of ID, this can be any photo ID which has not expired. **If you can't provide ID, you will not be allowed to sit the test.** You are also *not allowed* to bring in any electronic item, correction fluid or tape, erasable pens, paper, or any kind of container except a clear water bottle or clear pencil case.

The exam itself will be provided to you along with an answer booklet. The booklet itself is relatively short, only eight pages, but since you are just answering one question in one hour, that is generally plenty. You will also need to use that for the notes you take and any planning you want to do for your essay.

Generally, the test will be in the morning, in late October. The exact dates are released by Oxford fairly close to the time of the exam itself. If you are in school, then they will deal with registering you for the HAT and ensuring that all of your details are submitted properly.

If you are a mature or independent (such as home-schooled) student, you'll probably have to organise all of the arrangements yourself. This will include going to the Cambridge Assessment Admissions Testing website for the HAT, www.hatoxford.org.uk and registering for the HAT. This will include a fee (you only have to pay this if you are registering yourself, and you aren't registering as a student at a school).

When the invigilators start the exam, the majority of people sitting it won't start writing in earnest for some time. You should expect to spend a good amount of time reading and planning, and so your experience of the exam should normally be that you don't start writing until you're nearly halfway through the exam. At the end of the hour you'll hopefully have finished writing a couple of pages of text, and checked them over for mistakes, they'll be collected in and you'll be good to go, all done!

Access arrangements
If you are currently enrolled at school and taking the HAT, and you have specific access arrangements such as extra time, use of a computer, or screen-reader etc, then they should ensure that these are provided for you in the HAT as well. If you are sitting the HAT privately (for example as a mature student) you must ensure that you notify the test centre of your access requirements explicitly. Some test centres may require you to evidence these requirements, so make sure you notify them.

HOW TO SIT THE HAT, AND WHAT IT WILL BE LIKE – OVERSEAS

This section is only important for those applying to Oxford to study history-based subjects from outside of the UK.

If you are applying to study at Oxford while you are at school, your school may be able to help you arrange your test, or arrange it for you. Speak to the person at your school responsible for examinations, if there is one, and see what help they can give you. You may need to tell them about any access arrangements that you need and they may charge an additional fee for helping to organise the test.

If your school is not an authorised test centre, then they can apply to become one, though they may not choose to do this if you are the only applicant from your school who wants to go to Oxford for history. In the eventuality that your school is not an authorised test centre, you cannot take the HAT there and will have to take it at a location authorised by Cambridge Assessment Admissions Testing.

If you go to https://www.admissionstesting.org/find-a-centre/ and input your location, the website will show you the closest authorised test centre. The next thing you will have to do is contact them, using the information provided on the website, to book a test, pay any fees they may levy, and make access arrangements if you need them. Please note that your closest test centre may have an internal deadline for registering to take the HAT which will be sooner than the final deadline for registration shown on the HAT website. Make sure that you register as soon as possible with a test centre if you are studying overseas and your school is not one.

Some applicants choose to travel to the UK to take their HAT, in that case they will still need to register with a test centre in the UK. Once you have registered to take the test, make sure that you check with your test centre for when the test itself will be sat. You will need to make sure that you are at the test centre ahead of time, and if your test centre has particular requirements for proving your identity that you have the relevant evidence.

The exact experience in your testing centre may vary considerably based on where you are taking it, and you may be the only person sitting the test (though this is quite unlikely in many cases). However, your experience will be similar to those sitting the test in the UK. You'll be expected to take the test in exam conditions: no talking, no referring to notes etc. You will have one hour unless you have a disability or special requirement which means you get extra time for examinations and you have provided evidence of this to the test centre.

You'll be given two booklets in the exam, one will contain the question and extract, the other will be for writing your answer. This should be all the paper you need. You should only need one writing implement for the exam (we would recommend you use a black ballpoint pen) but bring a second one in case the first fails.

At the end of the test, your manuscript will be collected in and you will be dismissed. You won't be allowed to keep the question booklet, and your manuscript will be sent by fast post to Oxford, where they are all collected and marked.

HAT BASICS – HOW TO READ QUESTIONS

WHY DOES THIS MATTER?

One of the most important skills for any HAT student is reading questions. At first, this might seem laughably simple, but more students fail the HAT each year because they misread or misunderstood the question's requirements than any other single reason.

In the HAT, you will be presented with a question which says something like:

"What can we learn from this passage about the society in which the author lived?"

This is deceptively simple, and there are a number of ways in which the examiners writing your HAT paper will be trying to test your aptitude. Remember, the HAT is used as a filter, there are several tests that you must pass to meet the criteria required to be invited to interview. Reading comprehension is one of them.

At first glance, it looks like all you need to do to answer this question is read the passage and make a note of all the things the author says about their society and then put them in an essay. In fact, this question tells you that you have to assess the connection between the author and the passage, provide a robust definition of society, assess the passage for information concerning society as you have defined it, and judge the extent to which the existence, assumptions, and content of the passage can give you information about the society in which the author lived (which may not be the society which the author mentions in the passage).

A great candidate needs to be able to develop a list, like that, for whatever question they see, so that those can be used to inform their reading of the source, and their plan of action for the answer. In this section, we are going to walk you through how to take a question like the one above, break it down to its constituent parts, and use that to answer the question.

We'll also show you how to use that in your reading of the source. The source you get in the HAT will be quite long, and inherently complex. If you return to it after you have developed a good understanding to the question and read it through with that in mind it can allow you to notice connections and features you hadn't picked up on before. We will look at an example passage, and go through some examples of the kinds of connections you might find based on the question, and how you can make sure that you can duplicate that success in the HAT.

The last thing we are going to go through here is defining terms. This is technically something you'll have to do when you plan out your answer, but it actually has to be done at the reading questions stage so that you know just what you are looking for during your source analysis, which is up next. We're going to run through a few common terms in HAT questions, and how you can come up with definitions which suit you. In the above case, determining just what is meant by 'society' is incredibly important.

First, though, we need to look at how questions can be broken down into a simple statement of what you must do, and from there, the examiner's specific requirements can be determined.

SIMPLIFYING QUESTIONS

The way that you simplify questions for the HAT is first by determining what the **active elements** of the question are and using those to convert a question into an *instruction*.

Active elements are the components of the question which are variables in your consideration, or components which substantively change the requirements of the question. Let's look at some examples.

"What does this passage tell us about the political and cultural values of the author?"

"What does this extract tell us about the relationship between the Catholic church and the people of 16th century France?"

We have here two quite different questions which are both very similar to ones in previous HAT papers, and similar in format to the question you will see in your HAT exam.

"What does this passage tell us about..."
"What does this extract tell us about..."

These components use subtly different wording but are functionally the same. All they mean is that you should read the passage and write your answer based on what that can tell you, rather than based on any of your knowledge. These parts of the question do not constitute variables, you can only consider the passage, and you should never consider anything else. You will never be asked to consider anything else. While they do help establish the requirements of the question, they will be there in every single HAT question, they are static. This means that these parts are not active elements.

"The political and cultural values of the author?"

The rest of our first example question here brings in several different things at once. We now have specifics, we don't just have to read the passage, we have to read it and use it to discuss political and cultural values, we also know that we need to talk about the political and cultural values of a particular subject, in this case, the author. Therefore here, we have three active elements, they all change the requirements of the question beyond "read the passage", and give you an impression of what in particular they would like you to talk about.

"the relationship between the Catholic church and the people of 16th century France?"

This question is slightly different, but remember, the beginning is always going to be the same. There are several different active elements here, you are being asked to talk about a relationship, and it is a specific relationship, between two groups, the Catholic church, and the people of 16th century France. You also have an additional active element here in the form of a date range; a requirement of the question is established as being within the 16th century, and within France, while the passage may talk about those things alongside other places and times.

Active elements, then, are the parts of each question which determine the specific areas you want to investigate, you can recognise them because they all functionally change the question in some way beyond the original part, to read the passage, which we know will always be there. Try to identify all the active elements in the questions above, we have highlighted them below so try not to read further before trying it out!

When we revisit the above questions, the active elements that we can spot are:

"What does this passage tell us about the <u>political</u> and <u>cultural values</u> of the <u>author</u>?"

"What does this extract tell us about the <u>relationship</u> between the <u>Catholic church</u> and the <u>people of 16th century France</u>?"

Once we have identified the active elements, we can use those to convert the question into an instruction. Let's start with the first of our two examples.

"What does this passage tell us about the <u>political</u> and <u>cultural values</u> of the <u>author</u>?"

We know that the first part of every HAT question is just asking you to read the passage and write about it, so our instruction will begin with that every time. The rest of the instruction will be determined and altered by the active elements. So here, we know that we have to read the passage and respond to it by talking about political and cultural values held by the author. Converting this into an instruction gives:

"Read the passage, and write about the political values and cultural values that you think the author has, based on your reading.

The instruction is longer than the original question, but it is also much simpler, giving you a clear understanding of what you need to do, from which you can work out how to anticipate the examiner's requirements, read the extract, and plan out your answer. With the second example, the active elements are a little more complex.

"What does this extract tell us about the <u>relationship</u> between the <u>Catholic church</u> and the <u>people of 16th century France</u>?"

The question wants you to talk about a relationship, which can mean a range of things (you must decide what it means, we will cover how to do that in the defining terms section shortly). It also wants you to make sure that you talk about a specific relationship, between an institution (the Catholic church) and a population (the people of 16th century France). It is best if you can define things like 'relationship' when you are simplifying your question. Here, that would be:

"Read the passage, and write about the ways that the Catholic church influenced people, and vice versa, in 16th century France."

Let's look at one last example before we move on. The question:

"What does this passage tell us about the nature of power and royalty in 19th century Malawi?"

has the active elements:

"What does this passage tell us about the <u>nature</u> of <u>power</u> and <u>royalty</u> in <u>19th century Malawi?</u>"

And can become the instruction

"Read the passage, and write about the ways in which people in 19th century Malawi understood power and royalty to work."

USING THE QUESTION TO FIND THE MARK SCHEME

Once you've been able to identify the active elements of your HAT question, and simplified your question into instruction, you should be able to determine with some clarity what the examiner wants you to do.

HAT mark schemes vary in length and the level of prescriptive detail that they want you to go on, but there are several fundamental requirements which you must meet in order to secure a top-level answer, which is what you are going for! Those include a *perceptive reading of the passage to extract historical information surrounding the criteria they have given you*, to *efficiently communicate that information and where you got it from*, and to communicate, specifically, a *clear and unambiguous interpretation of what the past was like based on the passage*. These are always going to be there, but you can go further than that in your HAT preparation, and create for yourself a bullet-point list of the things the HAT examiners want you to do. Armed with that, you can plan out an answer which hits all of their 'high-level indicators' and maximise your chances of a great final mark.

The way that you can do this is to take the instruction you have developed from the original question, turn that into a set of distinct things that must be completed to satisfy the requirements of the question, and then apply the foundational HAT mark scheme essentials to them.

Let's start with a very simple question to examine turning the instruction into a set of things to complete, before moving on to a HAT question from the previous section.

Are cars the best way to travel?

You can turn this into the instruction: "Talk about whether or not you think cars are the best way to travel, and explain why" but you don't really need to, this is a hyper-basic question just for the sake of demonstration. This question is from a much more basic test than the HAT, so we know that they just want you to produce a balanced argument.

From this question, you can determine a few set things that you must do to answer it fully. Those include:

- ➤ Discussing the pros and cons of cars as a means of travel. This includes:
  - ○ what is good about cars, and
  - ○ what is bad about cars
- ➤ Discussing the pros and cons of alternative means of travel
- ➤ Assessing whether, based on this discussion, you think cars are the best way to travel
- ➤ Showing your thinking

In order to accurately answer the question above, you have to consider *both* whether cars are the best and not the best, as well as considering what other ways to travel might be better, and the reasons for that. You need to show the examiner that you have all the information, and you can be judicious without missing out pieces of information which don't agree with your point of view.

That means that in this next question,

"What does this extract tell us about the relationship between the Catholic church and the people of 16th century France?"

You know that you've got to consider *both* the way that the Catholic church affected people, and the way people affected the church, as a part of this 'relationship' That is why the question can be simplified to:

"Read the passage, and write about the ways that the Catholic church influenced people, and vice versa, in 16th century France."

From that, you know you need to:

- ➤ Talk about the way the Catholic church influenced the people of France
- ➤ Talk about the way the people influenced the Catholic church
- ➤ Determine what the passage can tell you about the relationship between the Catholic church and the people of 16th century France.

With what we know about *every* HAT mark scheme though, we can go further, we know that you have to extract historical information surrounding the criteria they have given you. That means *you must extract information about the ways the Catholic church influenced people, **and** the ways people influenced the church.* You also know that you have to communicate the source of all the information you have extracted, so you also *must refer back to the source to show your thinking behind each point you make about the relationship between the church and the people.* You also know that you have to give an unambiguous interpretation of the past, and by using the active elements in the question and its simplification you know that *you must make clear points about the relationship between the church and the people, and make informed statements about what that relationship was like in 16th century France specifically.*

For you to be able to do these things you've also got to perform some other steps, any additional steps also become mandatory components you must complete, so here, you need to define what is meant by relationship, in your answer, in order for you to be able to anticipate the mark scheme.

Therefore, if you had this question in the HAT exam, you could make reasoned estimates about the checklist that the HAT examiner will be using when marking your answer, and it might look like this:

- The candidate defines 'Relationship'
- They make unambiguous points about the relationship between the church and the people
- They make unambiguous points about the relationship between the people and the church
- They provide evidence for each of those points from the passage
- They focus exclusively on France in the 16th century.
- They reach definitive conclusions about what the relationship between the Catholic church and the people of 16th century France was like
- They ensure that these are organised into a piece of writing which makes sense

Two of these steps; that you need to provide evidence for each of your points, and that you need to ensure that the points are organised into a *piece of writing that makes sense* are also always going to be there, and are mandatory. It might help you to write them out in your plan anyway, but they are always going to be there, and you should try your best to remember them!

Let's bring down the other two examples we have looked at in this chapter, and you can practice with them. See if you can come up with a bullet point list like the one above for both of these.

"What does this passage tell us about the political and cultural values of the author?"

"What does this passage tell us about the nature of power and royalty in 19th century Malawi?"

A list for the first question might look like:

- Define 'political'
- Define 'cultural'
- Define 'values'
- Make unambiguous points about the political values of the author
- Make unambiguous points about the cultural values of the author
- Provide evidence for each of those points from the passage
- Focus exclusively on the author's own values
- Reach a definitive conclusion about the authors political and cultural values
- Ensure that these are organised into a piece of writing which makes sense

And for the second question:

- Define 'power'
- Define 'nature'
- Make unambiguous points about the nature of power based on the passage
- Make unambiguous points about the nature of royalty based on the passage
- Provide evidence for each of those points
- Focus exclusively on 19th century Malawi
- Reach a definitive conclusion about the nature of power and royalty in 19th century Malawi
- Ensure these are organised into a piece of writing which makes sense.

If your lists looked like these then you're on the right track. Once you have a list like this, then you have in your hands a guide to success in the HAT (both literally and metaphorically). The next step is using the list you have generated to guide your reading of the material.

USING YOUR LIST TO INFORM YOUR READING OF THE EXTRACT.

There is conflicting advice available online and from teachers about how best to apportion your time when it comes to reading the extract. The most common piece of advice is to always read the question first and then to turn to the extract, but in the HAT that doesn't make the most sense. The extract is central to your entire answer, and if you read it only once then you'll be referring back to it constantly, so you may as well read it twice. Here, we would recommend that the *first* thing you do in the HAT is read the extract. *Then* read the question, simplify it, and work out what the marking requirements are going to be, and *then* re-read the extract from top to bottom, bearing that scheme in mind as you go through it the second time.

When you conduct your second reading of the extract, there are several things you can look for that will make some of the steps in your list. First among those is the definitions if you need any. You should have a clear idea at this point what terms you will need to define because the question requires you to talk about them, and the meanings are either varied or ambiguous. When you conduct your second reading of the extract, make a note each time you read something in the passage that describes what you think of as the term you need to define. At the end of your reading, you will have a number of sentences describing that term, and you can use those as the basis for your definition. For example, consider the following extract from a passage, from which we need to find a definition of *status*:

Her marriage celebration <u>was greater than any other that had taken place at the palace, a celebration befitting the important status of her husband</u>. He was famous everywhere in the country for having co-operated with the British when they first arrived in Katsina. *At the time Muhammadu Dikko was not yet Emir but was known as a counsellor. Because of his success with the British colonial officers he was elevated to the status of Emir of Katsina.* **He saw to it that Ma'daki reached Katsina accompanied by her family's wealth; her slaves, her dowry, and her parents' gifts of grains and other foods** – corn, millet, rice, wheat, palm oil, groundnut oil, butter, etc. – for her new in-laws. Everything was loaded onto horses and camels because at the time there were no cars. After she reached Katsina another wedding celebration was held and this one was even bigger than the one held in Kano. Some years after the wedding the Emir decided to take Ma'daki *around the countryside to show her his domain*. After that he decided to take her everywhere he went.

And last but not least, we can see that his high status has been accompanied by considerable territory (countryside) under his control (domain)

<u>Occasionally, you'll get lucky and the passage will use the word you are trying to define. Here, high status means large celebrations and expenditure.</u>

Here, status is being discussed with notions of elevation. Status can change, and positions of power give higher status.

Here, we can see that the high-status Emir was marrying someone from a wealthy family, and so we can also draw a connection between status and wealth.

And here, we can see that the wedding between these two people of high status was larger than the largest one held at the palace mentioned at the start. Status equals public displays of wealth and control

From the passage, we can conclude that status has something to do with being wealthy, and from having access to abundant resources. It's also connected to public appearances, celebrations, and power. Dikko's status was increased when he was made Emir of Katsina. From this, we could create a definition of status which suits the passage, and therefore will give you the maximum applicability when writing out your answer. You can come up with your own definitions, but they might look something like *"Status is the public perception of the level of an individual's wealth, power, and control over others and their environment, higher status means higher levels."*

During your second reading, you can also use your list for other advantages. You can read the passage looking specifically for examples of the things you need to talk about (whether they are amorphous like 'status' or more specific, like the relationship between the Catholic church and the people of 16th century France). Highlight or otherwise note down all of the places in the passage where you can see that the author is talking about one of the points you have made in your list, and you'll be able to build up a much clearer idea in your head of what the source is trying to say, how you might be able to answer your question, and why the examiners chose this particular passage for the test.

When you are ready, practice this on some of the extracts in the sample questions provided at the end of this guide, or on HAT past papers available from the Oxford History Faculty website. See if you can create a list of mark scheme requirements from the question, and then re-read the passage, looking specifically for information which helps you make the points you need for a great answer!

DEFINING TERMS

We have already touched on ways that you can use the question to create a list of definitions you need to find, and how to re-read the extract with a view towards finding them, but the process can be challenging, and it is often a vital step in delivering a good answer to the question. One of the requirements HAT examiners have is that answers form a clear argument which makes sense. This is harder than you may think, and one of the main reasons that candidates fail to deliver this is by either not developing a solid definition of their terms, or developing one but never stating it in their response, so we are going to look at that briefly here.

Some questions will not require you to define any terms, because they will all be fairly self-evident, a question asking you to infer information from the passage about the financial wealth of the author, for example, doesn't need you to define 'financial wealth', because that has an unambiguous definition as it is. A question which asks you to define the 'cultural norms' of a city, however, is another matter. What does 'cultural' even mean? To get a good answer, you have to decide what it means. There is often no singular correct answer to this, what is important is that you choose a definition which allows you to make use of the material in the passage, and which makes sense to you. Any definition that does those things will be great, as long as you stick to it.

There is no way of knowing which terms will appear in your HAT, and we have already given you some tips in the previous section about how to use the passage to help you create your own definitions, but we have included here some example definitions of terms which have come up in recent HAT papers, as well as a few which could easily appear in yours. If you can, see if you can think of alternative definitions which you think are better, and add your own as you go.

Culture
"The collected knowledge, customs, and behavioural practices of individuals within a particular group or population."
Society
"An imaginary space in which people exist together through social interaction, either within a physical or intellectual territory, and where the majority favours abiding by shared rules"
Civilisation
"Any society characterised by either urban development or the formation of complex social structures, government, communications systems or shared technology"
Power
"The ability of an entity to influence the behaviour of others, or the surrounding environment"
Status
"The perception of the social position held by an entity or object within an established ranking"
Wealth
"The abundance of money or valuable possessions held by individuals or organisations"
Royalty
"People whose power is derived from royal status normally inherited from a King or Queen"
Religion
"A system of belief in a supernatural power or sacred things used to bind individuals together"
Relationships
"How two or more things or people are interconnected or behave towards each other"
Lives
"The collected, often regular or mundane, experiences of individuals or a social group."
Politics
"The activities and actions carried out by and between individuals and groups for the purpose of governing a physical or intellectual territory."
Art
"A collection of different creative outlets within a society, and the works that they produce with the intention of evoking an emotional response"

See if you can come up with definitions for any other terms you might like to add to this list. They will be incredibly valuable in your analysis and reading of the extracts.

HAT BASICS – HOW TO READ HAT PASSAGES

WHY DOES THIS MATTER?

It may seem obvious, but an incredibly important component of success in the HAT is reading the extract properly. Despite this, a huge number of candidates fail to do this properly each year. The HAT examiners that helped write this book talked particularly about the fact that many candidates damaged their final mark by writing about elements of the passage which they had misunderstood or misread, in other words, they had *gotten it wrong*.

This is what examiners call a 'low-level indicator' it's a sign that the candidate isn't performing at the highest levels required to make it through the filters. If you want to maximise your chances of an invitation to interview, you don't want any low-level indicators at all. One of the best ways to nip those in the bud is to make sure you read the extract well.

This means that you've got to make sure that you practice careful reading. There are some specific tips that this guide will give you momentarily, but above all of that, remember that you are the one that has to read the passage and you can't afford to misread it or miss stuff. In the exam, the stress of being timed, especially since time is so limited, can make candidates rush. Try to slow down, take your time to read the material, read the question, and then read the material again.

Misunderstandings are among the most common errors which derive from the way candidates read the extract. This can include things like identifying an artist as someone who paints, when in the passage they actually write poetry, or taking a question about kingship and trying to find evidence about the king's ship (which, unsurprisingly, did not go well). These are generally caused by rushing your reading and will be helped most by the section on careful reading, below.

Misreading is slightly different, it happens when a candidate understands the material, but misinterpreted a particular detail, like a beggar being forced to give up his horse, rather than his house. Small errors can lead to major misunderstandings about what the passage is saying, but they generally reveal themselves when you summarise the source because they tend not to make sense when considered with everything else. The sections here on understanding the central theme and taking notes will be particularly helpful.

Often one of the most difficult to fix, and tragic mistakes made in the reading of the extract is missing vital pieces of evidence or connections in the extract. Missing, for example, that the 'King's lauded brother' is the same person as the 'vile perpetrator of brutal fratricide' can entirely derail your answer, and is often not as a result of any misunderstanding or misreading, but simply not taking the time to think through the passage and analyse the source fully.

All of these are entirely avoidable errors and mistakes, and the subsequent sections containing basic tips on reading extracts, and survival essentials on things like source analysis will mitigate against those, but you must make sure that you give yourself the time to read, consider, annotate and analyse your text so that the answer you write contains great pieces of evidence.

CAREFUL READING

It's really important that you give yourself the time and space to make sure that your readings of the passage are careful, and considered. This may seem obvious to you, but it is where the majority of candidates fall down, so any good HAT guide needs to make sure this is covered.

In any HAT question, you will *always* find that the active elements, the parts of the question which you have been asked to focus on by the examiners, are present in multiple locations within the passage. We will look shortly at how to identify these pieces as you read through the passage, but in order to successfully apply the techniques which we are going to show you, it is first important to make sure that you can read carefully. You will not be able to get a good answer, or final mark for the HAT if you are unable to identify the majority of that content which relates to the topic(s) of the question. One of the fundamental tools you need to do this is being able to understand how the words, phrases, and sentences in the passage have been used to communicate what the author is trying to say. If you can do that, you can also understand more about *why* they have said it, which is incredibly valuable if you want to learn more information about what the author thinks about particular topics touched on in the passage, which your HAT question might be asking you about (things like 'religion' or 'society and culture').

To be a careful reader, you also need to make sure you pay close attention to the context in which words, phrases, or even entire sentences are being used. This is something which you can improve your skills in by learning how to identify the central theme of the passage and recognising the active elements as content in the passage, both of which we go onto next. It is important because a sentence in isolation might suggest a particular conclusion about one of the topics you are investigating, but as part of the larger whole, the meaning is transformed. This is something that can only be picked up through careful reading.

A useful trick if you want to make sure you are reading carefully is to develop a wide vocabulary. HAT passages will often contain explanations for particularly complex words, but not all of them, and if you have a good vocabulary then you minimise the risks of being unable to fully understand the passage. The best way to improve your vocabulary is simply by reading, try to read a diverse range of texts in English, incorporating both reference and creative texts, and keep a dictionary or thesaurus handy while you do so (there are plenty of online ones which work great on a phone or laptop as well).

Another thing you can do to help make sure you are reading carefully is to make sure that you pace yourself while you read. It is very tempting, in the pressure of the exam, to rush your way through the reading. Many candidates feel that the most important thing they can spend their time doing is writing, but it is better to write a shorter answer based on a careful reading, than a long answer full of errors and missed opportunities. Force yourself to take time to read through the passages. A useful technique you can employ here is to find a HAT passage from the examples at the end of this guide. Skim-read the text and time yourself. Once you have that time in mind, double it – that's the time you can use as a yardstick for your reading time on the HAT extract. If you are naturally a slow reader, then this may need tweaking. Guidance for how much time in total you should spend reading your HAT passage is detailed in HAT Survival Essentials – Essay writing – Timing on page 86 of this book.

If you have a guide time in mind, but you still find yourself rushing through parts or all of the passage when you practice, another technique you can try is 'reading aloud' in your mind, or sub-vocalising. By this, we don't mean speaking as you read (that would not be a good idea in the exam itself!) but taking the time to turn each word you read into the sound that it makes when spoken, in your mind. This will force you to read slower, and effectively listen to yourself saying the words of the passage. This technique is second nature for some, and harder for others, but for most of us it is how we first learn to read. Many people learn, or gradually stop themselves from subvocalizing as you grow up, but for careful analysis of text it can be incredibly useful as it helps your mind access the meaning of words and remember what you've read as you read through the passage.

The last thing to note here on careful reading is managing panic. Sitting exams is, for many people, an anxiety-inducing experience, and managing the anxiety you experience in the exam is really important to getting good results. We cannot, sadly, give you a quick solution to anxiety in this guide (no one can) but a useful tip that our very best performance coaches give to candidates is to remind yourself that worry is unproductive. If you are sitting in the exam, reading the passage and feeling worried, anxious, or panicked about performing well, about your final mark or about getting into Oxford, you are using up valuable brain capacity. The outcome you want, which is an interview and the offer of a place, becomes *less* likely the *more* you worry about it. This means that in the HAT, you want to try and actively remember that worrying, panicking, or rushing because you want to succeed, will only make you less likely to succeed. The key to success is to keep cool and stick to the plan you had before you came into the exam room.

HOW TO IDENTIFY THE CENTRAL THEME OF THE PASSAGE.

When you are faced with a passage as substantial as a HAT question, it's incredibly important that you can not only fully understand the meaning and nature of each sentence, each point and each piece of evidence. You also need to be able to understand the meaning of entire paragraphs. They are made up of several different sentences, each saying a different thing, but the sum of its parts usually has a clear meaning.

Each paragraph has its own meaning, but over and above that the entire piece will often be conveying a particular message, theme, or idea. Being able to identify this can be incredibly useful in determining the ways in which the passage is relevant to your particular question, and it also will reduce the opportunities for misunderstanding or misreading because you will be able to compare the arguments made in each individual sentence to the overarching point of the passage.

Not every passage in the HAT will have this kind of central theme. Some, like one of the examples later on in the book, are entirely documentary, but if the passage in your HAT consists of a narrative from a clear individual's point of view, it may well do, and you want to know how to identify it.

Identifying the overall message of the passage's author can also help *lend* new meaning to individual sentences or paragraphs in the passage which are hard to understand outside their bigger context, and this can be really helpful not only in avoiding mistakes but finding new connections.

When you are reading the passage, there are several things you can do to help you identify the central theme:

1. The first is to ask yourself what the passage's topic is. If the passage doesn't really have a topic, because it is something like an inventory, then it probably doesn't have a central theme. If you can identify a particular topic though, you may be on to something.

2. If you are struggling to determine whether or not there is a topic, try asking yourself whether there are any shared ideas or common motifs that permeate the passage, is there something which keeps coming up? If so, that will likely be the author's central theme. If there isn't, then it is unlikely that the passage has a central theme, and you should stop there.

3. From there, try to identify the author's feelings about the topic in question. Does it make them happy? Sad? Angry? It may not be possible to learn this, but even if not, it doesn't mean that the topic doesn't constitute the central theme.

4. Regardless of whether you could find value judgments pertaining to the topic in the passage, you can try asking yourself what the author of the passage was trying to do by writing it? More information on the ins and outs of this process are detailed in the later section on Nature, Origin, and Purpose (page 42).

5. Last but not least, once you've read the passage through, try to focus less on the detail, and more on the text as a whole. Ask yourself "what is this saying to me?" Try to consider the passage in its entirety, and you will have a much better chance of identifying its central theme.

If you can follow these steps, it should be possible for you to identify the author's central theme every time, which can really help your reading and understanding of the extract as a whole. You can also use the central theme, if there is one, to help you identify where the question's main active elements can be approached from.

RECOGNISING ACTIVE ELEMENTS FROM THE QUESTION AS THE THEME OF SENTENCES OR PARAGRAPHS IN THE PASSAGE.

Once you have simplified your question and found the mark scheme, you'll know what each of the main areas are that the examiners will want you to investigate (such as 'social values'). On your second reading of the passage, you'll be effectively looking for all the information available on each of those active elements.

The way that you do this is similar to the exercise we did above in the section on using the question to find the mark scheme. Run through each paragraph, looking for content which relates to the theme you are looking for. If there are multiple themes, some people find it easier to look for each one in separate read-throughs, meaning that you might do two separate readings following your unpacking of the questions. Some of this work seems a lot like common sense, but it is valuable to run through how to do it with an example so that you can be sure that your own technique is the one which will suit you best for the HAT.

This passage is taken from an ancient papyrus, describing a complaint to a local politician. The question for this question might be "What does this passage tell you about the treatment of **wealth** and **women** in Roman Egypt?" (This passage is a little longer than the previous example, but still much shorter than one you will get in the HAT. Its purpose here is to demonstrate a concept, not as a HAT practice paper.)

> To the most illustrious praefect, from Aurelia Artemis daughter of Paesius, of the village of Thraso in the Arsinoite nome. Conscious of your love of equity, my lord praefect, and your solicitude for all, especially women and widows, I approach you praying to obtain your aid. The matter is as follows. Syrion, who had become decemprimus of the aforesaid village of Thraso, persuaded my husband, Ganis by name, to pasture his sheep, this Syrion who has wrongfully appropriated my aforesaid husband's goats and sheep to the number of sixty; and so long as my aforesaid husband lived each enjoyed the fruits of his own property, my husband of his private flock and the aforesaid individual of his. Now when my aforesaid husband went the way of men, Syrion rushed in, wishing by means of his local power to carry off the property of my young children from the very bed of my husband and his body lying there. When I endeavoured to rescue our property and prepare my husband for burial, he drove me away with threats, and until this day he remains in possession of our flocks. Wherefore I entreat you, my lord, to send me an assistant by your command, in order that I may recover the property of my young children and of myself the widow and be able to comply comfortably with what is required of me. For my aforesaid husband was not detected in any fraudulent action touching the interests of the Treasury, but it is in the nature of the aforesaid Syrion to rob me the widow and my young children on every occasion, so that when he took the corn of my deceased husband for the corn-dues devolving upon me, as I was left without a helper, he gave no receipt. I appeal to you then, in order that by the appended direction of you the lord and kindly benefactor of all I may recover my property and be able to live with my young children in my own home and ever to vow my gratitude to your fortune. Farewell
>
> {Subscribed} The sacred year, 289. With a view to what is expedient for the revenues . . . his excellency the epistrategos shall sift the matter with the utmost equity.

We are looking for content which relates to the themes of *wealth* and **women**. See if you can read through the passage and make a note of all the content which relates to either of those things. Some of the content which you come across in your passage may concern multiple themes at once. In the version below we have highlighted all the applicable content, if any of it doesn't seem to be a connection to you, try considering the themes of the passage, and the implications of what each highlighted piece of content is saying.

To the most illustrious praefect, from **Aurelia Artemis daughter of Paesius**, of the village of Thraso in the Arsinoite nome. Conscious of your love of equity, my lord praefect, and **your solicitude for all, especially women and widows**, I approach you praying to obtain your aid. The matter is as follows. Syrion, who had become decemprimus of the aforesaid village of Thraso, persuaded my husband, Ganis by name, to pasture his sheep, *this Syrion who has wrongfully appropriated my aforesaid husband's goats and sheep to the number of sixty*; and so long as my aforesaid husband lived each enjoyed the fruits of **his own property**, my husband of his **private flock** and the aforesaid individual of his. Now when my aforesaid husband went the way of men, Syrion rushed in, wishing by means of his local power to carry off *the property of **my young children*** from the very bed of my husband and his body lying there. **When I endeavoured to rescue our property and prepare my husband for burial, he drove me away with threats, and until this day he remains in *possession of our flocks***. Wherefore I entreat you, my lord, to send me an assistant by your command, in order that I *may recover the property of my young children and* **of myself the widow and be able to comply comfortably with** *what is required of me*. For *my aforesaid husband was not detected in any fraudulent action touching the interests of the Treasury*; but it is in the nature of the aforesaid Syrion to rob **me the widow and my young children on every occasion**, so that when he took the corn of my deceased husband for the *corn-dues **devolving upon me, as I was left without a helper,** he gave no* **receipt**. I appeal to you then, in order that by the appended direction of you the lord and **kindly benefactor of all** I may ***recover my property* and be able to live with my young children in my own home** and ever to vow my gratitude to your fortune. Farewell

{Subscribed} The sacred year, 289. With a view to what is *expedient for the revenues* . . . his excellency the epistrategos shall sift the matter with the **utmost equity**.

There are several areas in the passage where the themes of wealth and women are both covered at the same time. If you have been able to identify many of these areas and note them down, then you are well on your way to creating a detailed breakdown of the source. The next step is identifying the relevance of each piece of content that you have identified to the question in your notes.

TAKING NOTES FROM YOUR PASSAGE.

If you read through the passage and recognise the active elements of the question in individual pieces of content, then in the HAT exam what you can do is underline or highlight the relevant pieces of text (a literal highlighter pen is probably the easiest way to do this, if you bring several colours you can assign each one to a different active element). As you do this, for each one you want to make a note of what that is telling you **as you go** to save time. The best place to do that is probably in the source booklet, which generally has a lot of blank space that is perfect for making notes.

These do not need to be detailed notes, just a brief summary of what you can learn from each one. To determine these, read through the parts of the passage which you have highlighted and for each one, ask yourself the same kinds of questions that you did when trying to determine the central theme of the passage. "What is this telling me?" "What can I learn from this particular section?" "What are the inferences that I can make based on this section?"

Again, this is largely a matter of common sense, but it can be difficult if you aren't experienced with careful reading of sources. We'll cover how to do this in detail in HAT Survival Skills – Assumptions from Content.

For now, it is important to make sure that you are comfortable with taking notes while you read the passage on your second read through, and that one of the key techniques to good extract reading is making notes as you go. The quality of these notes will only improve as you work through more of the Ultimate Guide!

HAT SURVIVAL ESSENTIALS
SOURCE ANALYSIS

The entire objective of the HAT could be summed up as 'source analysis.' The HAT writers give every candidate the same source and compare their ability to analyse that source and communicate the results of their analysis. There are a huge number of different skills which source analysis requires, and it is important that you are familiar with all of these, can use them effectively on unseen test papers.

There is a massive range of potential sources which you might be presented with in the HAT. No one can cover all of the different possible types, let alone the individual examples from each. What that means is that, instead, you need to learn abstract skills, ones which you can apply to any source and generate your own insightful, valuable conclusions.

PRIMARY OR SECONDARY?

One of the most fundamental components of source analysis, but one which is overlooked by many candidates (and teachers) is how to determine whether a source is primary or secondary. This can influence your interpretation of the source in several ways. A primary source will often give you a lot more information about context, about how people felt and acted at the time you're being asked about in the HAT. A secondary source, on the other hand, can include information from a wider range of people, and give you more information about people's motivations and the consequences of their actions. Secondary sources are rarer than primary sources as choices for the HAT, but they are certainly not an impossibility for your upcoming HAT exam.

Primary sources are ones which are written by people who were direct participants in or eye-witnesses of what they are describing, and they usually date from the period they describe. These sources can often be incredibly useful both for what they actually tell us about the events described, but also what we can infer about the assumptions and worldview of the author from what they have said, and how they chose to say it. On rare occasions, you will get primary sources which are written much later, such as someone describing their childhood while they are in their eighties. As these are written long after the events described, it might be easy to think that these are secondary sources, but because they are written by someone who was present during the events described in the source, they are providing an authoritative report on the subject, and it remains a primary source.

Some examples of primary sources include:

- Government documents
- A transcript of a speech or interview
- Autobiographies
- Official documents (transcripts of court proceedings, inventories, birth and death certificates)
- Diaries
- Letters
- Newspaper articles (from the time you are learning about)

Often, resources like textbooks, journal articles, magazine articles, or any work written after the events they describe are considered to be secondary sources automatically by students (sometimes even by teachers). It is important to stress that this is not true, and these are not rules that you can apply to sources in order to determine whether they are primary or secondary. For example, a textbook written about computer graphics in 1980 is a primary source if you are studying the history of computer graphics in the 1980s. This is because sources like that can tell us a huge amount about the state of affairs at the time, about the way people thought, felt, and acted in relation to the topics they relate to at the time that you are investigating as an historian, both in a HAT exam and more broadly in your historical research at university.

Secondary sources are very different in that they generally combine information from a range of different sources to provide analysis or other commentary on the events that you are studying. They can sometimes incorporate or otherwise refer to primary sources but were created after the events which you are studying, and will always have a particular point or argument which the author is trying to make.

Some examples of secondary sources include:

- Journal articles
- Academic dissertations
- Opinion pieces
- Literary or artistic critiques
- History textbooks
- Encyclopaedias

Remember that any one of these sources can be used as a primary source for very specific areas. An encyclopaedia, for example, is a secondary source if you are studying any of the things described in it, but an encyclopaedia from the 1920s is also a primary source if you are studying the history of something like education, bookmaking or even encyclopaedias themselves. In general though, you can recognise a secondary source because it has a particular argument which the author is advancing, or it is collecting information from a wide range of sources for the purpose of teaching the reader something.

In the HAT, you will generally be able to recognise whether a source is primary or secondary by examining whether it refers to other sources (secondary) or whether it is describing an event or period (primary). All of the examples we have provided at the end of this guide are from primary sources, because Oxford hasn't used a secondary source for the HAT since at least 2007, but it is important to be able to recognise them so that you can identify the source you are given with authority.

As a result of this weighting though, we wanted to ensure that the information you had was as useful as possible, so we have focused from here on out on analysing primary material (although a lot of this is still applicable to secondary source analysis as well!)

NATURE, ORIGIN, AND PURPOSE

In GCSE and A-Level history, you may have already come across teachers, assignments, or specifications which refer to the Nature, Origin and Purpose of sources. These are fundamental components of source analysis, and if you can learn to identify each of these for sources as you see them, it can have a significant impact on your ability to understand just what the source in your HAT is about. If you can understand these things about the source, you will also be able to demonstrate those through your analysis, and the HAT examiners are looking for candidates who are capable of reading historical sources and determining what they are doing.

You'll never get a question in the HAT asking you "what is the origin of this source" or anything like that, but learning how to determine the nature, origin, and purpose of sources can really help you draw conclusions and interpret the source in a way that is valuable to the question you are asked, as we'll see in more detail below.

Nature

Put simply, the nature of the source is what it is. Often, in the HAT, you will be given some information about the source in the exam booklet which you might be able to use to determine the nature. For example, you might be told that the source is something like "a page from Homer's, *The Odyssey*, first written in around 800 BCE, describing the titular character Odysseus's interactions with his wife, Penelope." From this, and the extract itself, you will need to see what you can determine about the nature of the source.

It is important to remember here that when you are writing your answer to the HAT question, you must not bring in any of your own knowledge. This means that the limits of what you can talk about concerning the source you are given in the HAT are defined by what you have been told, and what you can reasonably infer about the nature of the source from the source itself, which is often extremely limited, so the information which you are given is among the most important.

Determining the nature of a source is often a matter of common sense. What you need to do is consider what you have been told about it, and what it looks like. A really useful exercise is to examine the source and the information you have been given, and trying to visualise what you think the original version of the source looks like, rather than the version you have in the test. In this case, you've been told it is from *The Odyssey*, and you'll have a page or two of poetry as your extract. From this then, you can determine that the source is literary in nature, it is taken from a poem, and that it is showing the relationship between a husband and wife.

You may well be given more information than that, in which case you should use it to your advantage. Some HAT exams will provide a considerable paragraph of information about the nature of the source, its origin, its content, and even who wrote it. All of this information can be useful, but for now we will focus on the nature of the source.

In our example here, you know that the nature of the source is literary, and taken from an ancient poem we also know that it focuses on a particular individual, Odysseus, based on the fact that the title is seemingly derived from his name. From this, there are several things that we can determine. The source might, for example, rely fairly heavily on artistic license, since it is a literary work. We don't know whether it is a work of fiction, but any elements in the text which appear particularly far-fetched could be explained in that way.

You also know that the source is a description of the interactions between a husband and wife, that means that it can give you valuable information about perceptions of different gender roles in the society which created the work, and information about the way that marriages were depicted. Questions asking about cultural values, social values, or gender dynamics would all work well with a source like this, and you know from its nature that there will be material in the source which you can use to learn about the ways in which the author understood those kinds of factors.

Because it is a poem, you could also use it to talk about art forms, which might be useful in a question about society or culture. You know that poems were written at the time and that they were clearly quite long, as you know that this is just an excerpt from a larger piece. You could reasonably infer from that that poems were used as a component of storytelling as a result.

Just what useful information you can derive from a source, based on its nature, depends on the exact question that you are given, but the HAT examiners will certainly want you to use the nature of the source to your advantage, so make sure that you bear it in mind, and that you practice at quickly identifying the nature of sources.

To summarise: the nature of a source is what it is, you can work out the nature of the source from the information given to you in the exam, and from the content and structure of the source by asking yourself what you could work out about what the source might have looked like before it was copied into your exam. It is useful for answering a range of HAT questions, but will never be the topic of a question on its own.

Origin

While the nature of the source is what it is, the origin is where it is from. There are two main strands of 'origin' that you might want to interact with, one is fairly simple, the geographic and temporal location, when and where in the world was the source created? This might be information you are given, but you can't rely on it. The other strand of origin is slightly trickier to figure out, and that's to do with who created it. Again, you may be told about the author, and what the author did, but again, this is not something that can be guaranteed.

For example, you could be presented with a source for which you are told it was

> **"Written by Gregory, a clergyman from Cologne and philosopher and sent to a contact of his, Rasmus, in Sweden."**

From this, you can determine that the origin of the source was Cologne. You don't know when though. You can also determine that it was written by Gregory, and the letter itself was recovered from Rasmus's possession, so it had travelled to Sweden before being preserved and eventually transcribed into your exam for you. Can you think of other things you can learn from that information about the origin?

Once you have everything you can glean from the information you've been given, there are also things you can learn from the content of the source itself. For example, the first paragraph reads:

"My dearest Rasmus,
I wish you the very greatest wellbeing and contentment as you work in the Lord's name. I learned of the troubling encounter that you had with the local savages and endeavoured to contact you at once. Sadly, I could not until recently as I was unable to secure a scribe for this letter, nor a courier to convey it to you. With the lessening of winter, however, I have been able to secure both, and I am delighted to once again correspond with you on these matters of great import to our great church."

From this, we can determine several points about the source's origin specifically. We know that the source originated from a person who was a personal acquaintance of the recipient and that it was written as a letter (this touches on the nature as well, but it is important to note that the source originated from correspondence exchanged between two people.) We also know that it was written by and sent to clergymen, so it may have been kept by Rasmus or potentially the church we know they shared (from the very last sentence). We can also tell from Gregory's mentioning of 'a scribe for this letter, nor a courier to convey it' that Gregory was, most likely, not the person who actually wrote the letter at all, it was written by someone else, and that it was written in a place where access to scribes and couriers was limited, and possibly even seasonal. Gregory also makes mention of the lessening of winter, so we can infer that this letter was written in the spring or summer and that this source was written in response to a letter which Gregory may have received from Rasmus, or indeed someone else but concerning something that happened to Rasmus.

From the content of the passage in the HAT, combined with the information which the examiners have given you, you've been able, then, to work out quite a lot of information about the origin of the source. The value of this depends on the question that you are being asked, but origin is generally very useful for talking about what you can learn about the society or civilisation which produced the source in question. You can use the analysis you have done of origin to talk about the fact that this was a civilisation in which not everyone has the ability to write, that letters are transported by hand, that there is a church which is shared across quite a large area and that people within that church correspond by letter irregularly and infrequently. All of this has come from a single paragraph and is the beginning of a considerable body of evidence which you can make use of to respond to a range of different questions.

In summary: the origin of the source is where it comes from, and also who wrote it. You can work it out from the information given to you in the exam, and from what the passage actually says (if anything) about its own creation. It is useful for answering a range of HAT questions, particularly because it tells you about the author, but will never be the subject of a question on its own. (The importance in understanding the author's nature will be covered more fully in the section on authorship on page 51)

Purpose.

The purpose of a source can be best summed up as "what did the author want to achieve by writing it?" It is far less likely that you will be given direct access to information like this by the HAT examiners. You will probably have to get it from the passage itself. Understanding the purpose can be very valuable because it can help highlight the existence of possible biases or other limitations of your source, which in turn can help you answer questions about society, culture, or more specific questions about the role of particular individuals.

The best way to work out the purpose of the source is to consider what you already know about the nature and the origin and combine them. Based on that information, you should be able to tell who wrote it, and who the intended audience was. In the case of our first example, we know that it was a poem, and the intended audience was any number of people who would be expected to listen to and understand the poem. In the second example, we know exactly who the audience was meant to be, Rasmus, the clergyman.

By combining these, we can begin to identify purposes. If we take the above letter from Gregory to Rasmus, for example, we know that both of the named individuals in the source are members of the same church and that Gregory sought to check that Rasmus was well following an incident with 'local savages':

> "My dearest Rasmus,
> I wish you the very greatest wellbeing and contentment as you work in the Lord's name. I learned of the troubling encounter that you had with the local savages and endeavoured to contact you at once. Sadly, I could not until recently as I was unable to secure a scribe for this letter, nor a courier to convey it to you. With the lessening of winter, however, I have been able to secure both, and I am delighted to once again correspond with you on these matters of great import to our great church."

Because we know that this was a letter sent from Gregory to Rasmus, we know that one purpose was to communicate, particularly, to learn information from Rasmus. Rasmus took the time to wait for a scribe and a courier in order to send the letter, so clearly that was quite important to him. We also know that this source originated within, and was sent to members of a church who are existing in the context of 'local savages' at least in Rasmus's case. We could also then infer that an ancillary purpose of the letter was to reinforce Rasmus's belief in the greatness of their church and that Rasmus was working in the Lord's name, in other words, he was trying to reassure Rasmus. This is useful to you, as it means that you can determine further information about the author, and the world in which they lived, which is often the subject of questions you are asked in the HAT.

The other valuable thing which purpose can give you, mentioned above, is information about bias. Bias is inevitable in almost all sources, but what matters is being able to show to the examiner that you are able to recognise it and mitigate against it. When you are considering what sources of bias there may be in a passage, the purpose can help you with this. Is the source trying to persuade the audience of something? Is the audience going to be someone likely to be in a position of power over the author? If you can determine who wrote it, and who they wrote it for, you should be able to give yourself a great shot at determining what the range of reasonable sources of bias can be expected from this particular passage *in a vacuum*. You can then mitigate against that by explicitly mentioning your awareness of it, and potentially even using the existence of that bias to make a point about existing power structures at the time that the source was created!

COMMON DIFFICULT SOURCE TYPES, AND WHAT THEY CAN TELL YOU

While we can't give you a walkthrough of every single source type in the HAT, we've given you the tools needed to determine the nature, origin, and purpose of any source that you find. In order to help give you some clearer structure for how these work, we're now going to run through some of the most common source types that you find in the HAT. While no one can guarantee what will show up, these are among the most common, and will also give you a valuable tool for understanding more about how sources work, and this will not only help you in the HAT but beyond that in the other history work you undertake in future.

Legal documents

Legal documents have appeared as sources in the HAT several times in the past, examples include the 2014 and 2016 papers. They are often chosen by examiners because there is no clear agenda, and the origin can be quite hard to pin down.

They are challenging sources because legal documents are largely descriptive, with very little 'flavour' for candidates to latch on to, but they can also be very rewarding in terms of HAT exams. Because legal documents so rarely directly interact with the world around them, the amount of information that you can learn is inherently quite limited. One of the first things (which so many people skip over) in these kinds of questions comes from the existence of the document itself. This is always a factor which people should consider, but with legal documents, their existence tells you about a shared legal system, potentially about the existence of courts, lawyers, judges. It also tells you that there is a system of writing, document storage, record keeping, and legal obligations in the society which produced the source.

Legal documents in the HAT will often focus on the treatment of a specific subset of individuals. In the 2014 paper, it was beggars, and in 2016 it was slaves. If you are given a legal document in your HAT, the chances are that it will be a document describing aspects of how the law pertains to a particular demographic group within a society. These documents then can also:

- Give information on what people can and cannot do
- Give information on how people are separated into different groups
- Give information on how crimes are punished
- Give information on how crimes are judged
- Give information on the subjects of the law (and those who are above it)
- Give information on the events or beliefs which necessitated the existence of the laws mentioned in these documents

In terms of your ability to work with passages from legal documents in the HAT, it is also important to bear in mind that while they may reflect unjust laws, prejudices, or incorrect assumptions, the sources themselves is an *extremely reliable* indicator of what the legal system of the time looked like. Legal documents will very, very rarely be seeking to persuade or deceive their audience of anything. The audience of these kinds of sources can vary wildly, but the purpose is generally to instruct people, or otherwise state 'facts'.

Survival tips:
- Remember that any legal document tells you something about the state which created it
- Remember that 'authorship' is often hard or impossible to determine, and you should focus instead on who the document is targeting, and what that tells you about the world that created the passage
- Such documents are often trying to combine several different groups' agendas into a single legal code or set of laws and so to get the most out of legal sources, you need to always identify the purpose of the passage, and from there how it reflects on its surrounding environment

Spoken transcripts

Transcripts, and their related sources oral histories, are often highly complex and rich sources. They can be chosen by HAT examiners because they require a lot of you as a test candidate. One of the main limitations in oral histories specifically is that they date from some time after the events described (often a considerable time) and so there is an issue with the author misremembering things.

When it comes to transcripts, there are two main forms: shorthand notes and stenographic or recorded transcripts. The latter are much more accurate, they are usually based from a record made in real-time and will generally be verbatim copies of what was said. Note based transcripts tend to be 'representative' of what was said, not accurate representations, there is a greater margin for error.

From both types of spoken sources, they can cover almost any topic, but they often have a different tone from written sources, so be prepared for oddly arranged sentences, poor grammar, or strange turns of phrase.

One of the things to really remember is that these sources were all, originally, things people said, so there is a huge amount of information we are missing from the audience, as the reaction of the audience has a huge influence on how many people speak.

Transcripts can be incredibly valuable, however, because they always give a firsthand account, not only of what occurred but what people were saying. This is important because we can learn about:

- The things which the author thought it important to emphasise
- Ways that the author sought to describe events, people, or concepts
- Ways that the author believed their audience would feel or think
- The way that the author thought, at the time they spoke

These can, more than many other primary sources, give us clear insight into the way that people thought and felt at specific moments in the past. In the HAT, sources like this may be used to ask questions about social values, the style of someone's leadership, or cultural elements like power or status.

Survival tips:
- Spoken sources give you direct access to what the author told other people at a specific time and place, so you can use this to learn about what they valued, and what they felt was important to communicate

- What they are saying may not be what they want their audience to hear, so pay attention to any notes about the audience's reaction, "I know you do not wish to hear this" or "Please, hold your applause"
- What the author said was not, necessarily, the same as what they thought. As you cannot bring in external knowledge, you must admit this limitation and work around it. You can argue that what they said implies that they believed it, but you must be careful making claims about beliefs based solely on the content of their statements

Letters

While there are a huge range of different possible subjects for letters, they are a comparatively simple source to analyse. Letters, generally, have one author and one recipient, an audience of one. This means that it can be easy to work out the origin and purpose of letters based on their content. As letters are almost always private, you can make some assumptions about what it can tell you:

- The author is less likely to be seeking to deceive the audience than in more public sources, so it can give you a more accurate reflection of the author's thoughts and feelings
- It can tell you about the fact that correspondence was exchanged between people in the context they shared (which can be very limited)
- Letters had limited size and length, so what they chose to write about can tell us what was important to the author. What information are they communicating, or requesting etc?

Some letters can be public, this can include open letters, letters to newspapers, or letters between senior political figures (especially from the last century) with these, a lot of the usual rules for letters don't apply, as there is more often an assumption that the author is seeking plausible deniability, or to be more directly persuasive and/or deceptive.

In the HAT, letters are often used by examiners to ask questions about society. Their privacy means that people often shared more intimate information, or indeed casual information about their lives which they wouldn't think to mention had they recorded an oral history or chronicle, for example. You can generally approach letters as a reliable indicator, both of the author's own beliefs and of the world which they describe. In some cases (like the infamous 2015 paper about the 'dog-headed' ones) you will have letters which are responding to second-hand information which the author cannot verify. Remember that if the author can't verify it, neither can you, but even this kind of information is still useful, as you know that the author lives in a world in which people can believe fantastical things to be true.

Survival tips:
- Consider both the author and the recipient when weighing up the content of a letter. A letter to or from children may well have a very different purpose and level of accuracy in its depictions of the world or daily life than one between adults
- You can quickly work out the origin and purpose in letters, so give yourself extra time to analyse the content and answer the question
- People rarely lie in letters, if they are saying something you believe to be false, the first thing to consider is that they are unaware that it is false. Doing this might let you talk about the kind of world they live in in order for this belief to exist, which is the kind of high-level thinking examiners love

IDENTIFYING LIMITATIONS – AND HOW DOES THIS CHANGE YOUR ANSWER?

In the recent sections, we've briefly referred to limitations and biases in the source. There is not much that needs to be said about reliability itself, because in the HAT you only have one source and you cannot use your own knowledge, so the source they have given you must be the sole source of information.

However, the best HAT candidates must show that they can recognise the limitations of a source, and respond to them, work around them, and show the examiners that they are able to produce valuable conclusions, even from sources which, on the face of it, have very little to offer. To that end we are going to look at an example of a 'problem source'. We'll then identify its limitations, and see just how many of them we can turn to our advantage.

This source was written by Gregory, bishop of Tours, in the late 6th century AD, and describes events 90 years before in a territory governed by the descendants of Clovis, one of the main figures in the passage.

> While Clovis[1] was in Paris, he sent secretly to Chloderic, the son of Sigibert[2], saying 'Your father is old. If he were to die, his kingdom would come to you of right and my alliance would come with it.' Chloderic was led astray by his lust for power and began to plot his father's death. He set assassins on him and had him murdered, so that he might gain possession of his kingdom. By the judgement of God, Chloderic fell into the same pit that he had dug for his father. He sent messengers to King Clovis to announce his father's death. 'My father is dead,' said he, 'and I have taken over his kingdom and his treasure. Send me your envoys and I will gladly hand over to you anything that you may care to select from this treasure.' 'I thank you for your good will,' answered Clovis. 'I ask you to show all your treasure to my messengers, but you may keep it …' [The envoys came, saw the treasure and encouraged Chloderic to finger the gold in a chest] As he leaned forward to do this, one of the Franks raised his double-headed axe and split Chloderic's skull. This unworthy son thus shared the fate of his father. When Clovis heard that both were dead, he came to Cologne himself and ordered the inhabitants to assemble. 'Chloderic, the son of your King, my brother, was plotting against his father and putting it out that I wanted him killed. As Sigibert fled, Chloderic had him murdered. While Chloderic was showing his father's treasure, he in turn was killed by somebody or other. I take no responsibility for what has happened. It is not for me to shed the blood of one of my fellow kings, for that is a crime. But since things have turned out this way, you should turn to me and put yourselves under my protection.' The men of Cologne clashed their shields and shouted their approval; they raised Clovis on a shield and made him their ruler. Thus he took over both the kingship and the treasure and submitted Sigibert's people to his own rule. Day in day out God submitted the enemies of Clovis to his dominion and increased his power, for he walked before him with an upright heart and did what was pleasing in his sight.

---

[1] A Frankish king, based in Paris, and recently converted to Christianity
[2] King of the Franks in modern Germany

The first thing you should do is try to determine just what the limitations of the source are and make a note of them. When that is complete, return to this point and see whether you found some we didn't mention.

So the first thing we know here comes from what we've been told about the source, which is similar to the level of detail you may be provided by the examiners in the HAT. You know that the source was written almost a century after the events described. That means that we've got one limitation straight away – the source may not be an accurate reflection of events at the time, as the author was not an eyewitness. Another limitation also comes from this information at the top, that the author, Gregory of Tours, lived and worked in a land controlled by Clovis's descendants. It should be obvious what limitation that poses, there is a risk of bias. The end of the passage is particularly odd, because it jumps from an unflattering description of Clovis's deception to explaining that he was pleasing in the sight of God. This may well be because the author had to make it clear that he thought Clovis to be a great figure as doing otherwise may have jeopardised his position.

Another limitation is hinted to us from the first note about Clovis, in which we are told that he was a recent convert to Christianity. The author, also a Christian, would be influenced to some extent by his subject's shared religion and this could colour the way in which Clovis was described.

Both of these limitations need to be addressed in order for you to show the HAT examiners that you are able to work on sources with such limitations. The first and most important step in doing this is simply acknowledging them. Say something like

"While much can be learned from this source, it must also be recognised that the source has limitations, chiefly that Gregory was writing in a land governed by Clovis's descendants, and could, therefore, be directly or passively manipulated to depict Clovis in a way which benefited his rulers. A second limitation is that Clovis was a recent convert to Christianity, and Gregory a Christian bishop, their shared religion may serve to limit the extent to which Gregory's retelling of Clovis's story can be considered accurate."

You can then demonstrate how you are going to work around this, it does not need to be long and complex, merely an acknowledgement of your ability to consider those limitations as part of the source, and even an advantage:

"As a result, this may lend some explanation to Gregory's unusual last sentence and might hint at the existence of power structures correlating kingship to family history, and the value of religious acceptance to the Frankish population."

Specifically, the shortcomings in this source can yield the following points:

- One influence is Gregory's Christianity - Christianity is growing, and having a Christian identity is something which leaders value, as it improves their image. Religious faith can be very serious, and can drastically change the way in which actions can be justified.
- Another influence is the descendants of Clovis. Gregory exists as a senior religious figure in a town controlled by Clovis's descendants - State leaders have some control over religious institutions. Thus, one can infer that control over religion confers some level of power. Similarly, we can see a connection between religion and suitability to rule - Clovis's descendants care that their ancestor is seen as righteous.
- The time gap - message has survived for nearly a century, words and messages have been preserved.

If you can recognise where potential limitations and sources of bias can be, and use those to better understand the material that you're being presented with, then you can hit more of the high-level indicators required to really excel.

AUTHORSHIP

Authorship can be a complex issue in the HAT, and knowing how to deal with it and what areas you may want to consider when discussing authorship in your response can be very useful.

The first thing to address is just what we mean by authorship. Simply, authorship is who wrote the passage you are reading. This is subtly different from the Origin, which is a combination of the location, time, institutions, and people who created it. With Authorship, we just want to examine the person who wrote it, as very often that is crucial to your answer.

The author is so important because, in the vast majority of HAT questions, regardless of whether you are being asked about the author's opinion or not, their opinion is actually all you have. The vast majority of sources for the HAT will have a clear single author, and they will be writing about something they have seen or heard. This means that their opinions, thoughts, beliefs, prejudices, and knowledge will be encoding everything that they talk about. That is the most important thing about authorship, and if you can learn to recognise and work with it, it can drastically improve your HAT responses.

Those opinions and beliefs about the author's world and society are what we call the Author's Sphere. It's the sum total of their universe, as they know it and understand it. There are a lot of things that we can assume to be within that sphere, like their own opinions and beliefs, the actions that they are describing from eyewitness experience and their interaction with whatever format their thoughts are being recorded into (be it a camera, a microphone, a computer, a typewriter, a piece of paper or another person etc).

Things inside the author's sphere can be treated by you as *accurate* representations of what the author *believed*. You never have to take them as the truth, just that it is likely true that the author *believed* what they said to be true. Let's consider this very short excerpt from a HAT passage as an example.

"As it transpired, the people of this town all rejoiced when they learned the news of your imminent return, though I was quick to counsel them that the journey would yet be long, though with prayer and piety your eventual return would be assured in the eyes of the Lord God."

We have examples here of the author talking about things that are within his sphere – the behaviour of the people of the town in which he lived, and with whom he interacted, as well as his belief that there was a God to whom one could pray and expect results. We don't have to assume or argue that these things are true, but we should argue that the author believed them to be true, and this can reflect either the author's own beliefs or the beliefs of people living where the author lived at the time.

If we consider the following sentence from the same passage, we can see an example of information from outside of the author's sphere.

"Privately, I was concerned that the delay in your return had been wrought by the witchcraft or other machinations of the hags you described in your previous letter."

Here, information within the author's sphere is their concern about the delay and the fact that they had received a letter previously. They also mention 'hags' who were practising witchcraft or had some other means of delaying the arrival of the person. The author knows nothing about these 'hags' or their witchcraft beyond what was relayed to them in the letter they received. It lies outside their sphere. We can't, then, say that they believed witchcraft to be occurring, but we can say that they believed witchcraft to be possible.

There is also information which lies outside of the author's sphere. This is information which they are reporting based on second-hand information, such as from a letter, rumour, or things they have heard from others. It can also include assumptions they have made about the causes of things which they cannot secure direct evidence for. In these cases, what we need to do with this kind of information is different. We cannot assume that they believed it to be true, but we *can* assume that they lived in a world in which such things were plausible and worthy of record.

Another element of authorship which we need to consider is the influences upon them. This has already been touched on in the example we gave for the limitations of the source, where Bishop Gregory was influenced by Clovis's descendants and by the church. What recognising influences on the author can do is help you explain *why* the author believes certain things, or has particular opinions.

Once you have identified the author's voice, and their sphere, you can use the information that you are given in the HAT to determine how they may be influenced, what external factors may drive them. Let's look at this excerpt from a HAT passage to demonstrate.

This extract is taken from a chronicle of St Alban's Abbey, written by a Christian monk based there called Thomas. Read it and see if you can work out what influences there may be on Thomas's writing and how this might shape your analysis of what he can tell you about the world around him.

"Abbot Hugh caused a new crucifix to be made for the monastery church, whereupon the sculptor carved no specially beautiful or important feature except upon holy days only on which days he himself fasted on bread and water. Moreover he had a naked man before him to look at, that he might learn from his form and carve the crucifix all the fairer. When this crucifix was set up, the Almighty constantly wrought many solemn and manifest miracles through it."

Hopefully, you are already beginning to see that there could be a couple of influences on the author. Can you also identify whether this account is from within the author's sphere or outside of it?

One influence is hinted at by the description you are given of the source. You know that the author is a Christian monk, and he is writing about a Christian institution, an Abbey, which also happens to be where he is based. This means that the wishes of the people, possibly even Abbott Hugh himself, will be influencing the author. Another potential influence, or at least an ancillary influence, is also apparent here; he is based at the monastery, so we can assume that he was invested in it being successful. A monastery in possession of a crucifix so fair that it manifests miracles would be a great draw for visitors and donations, so he or others in the monastery may have sought to overemphasise the power of the crucifix in order to secure interest.

We can also see that Thomas's religion is playing a part. He talks about 'solemn and manifest' miracles being wrought through the crucifix in the monastery church, which is within the author's sphere, and so we can say that the author clearly believes miracles to have taken place.

We can make use of the extract, and what we are told about it, to work out what things may have influenced the author at the time, and shaped what they believed or what they said. They don't necessarily have to be the same thing as limitations, and can certainly be approached differently, but a good exercise for people wanting to practice this skill would be taking individual paragraphs from the extracts in this book or elsewhere and trying to identify all the limitations, and the author's sphere and influences upon them.

HAT Survival Tip: 'Unknown unknowns' – a lot of students trip up when considering the Author's sphere and what lays outside of it, and argue that because the author has not mentioned something, this means that it must not have existed, or been true. You can't ever make these assumptions, as they rely on external knowledge. Arguing that "the author makes no mention of atheists, which means that there were no atheists in the author's time" can't work, because you could use that to explain everything, and so it isn't a valid unit of analysis.

SEPARATING STATEMENTS OF FACT FROM STATEMENTS OF OPINION, *OR:* WHAT THE AUTHOR KNOWS VERSUS WHAT THEY *THINK* THEY KNOW.

As in the examples above, we can identify several areas which are the opinion of the author, rather than absolute facts. As far as the author is concerned, it seems likely that they considered some things to be truths while others were just their opinion. If the author talks about a crucifix wreaking miracles, that is (to them) a fact, while if they talk about being concerned that a friend was delayed in their return home by witchcraft, that is an opinion. They do not know that witchcraft is to blame, merely that it could be.

It can be very useful to recognise the difference between statements of fact and opinion in texts, as facts can tell you about the ways that people knew the world to be, while opinions can be used to demonstrate superstitions or, at least, part of a *wider range* of potential views or ways of knowing the world.

In the modern world, we only assume things to be true, generally, if they can be proven. This means that, when considering things like Thomas's description of miracles above, we might reason that this cannot be a fact because miracles cannot be proven.

It is important to remember that the way that we know the world is not the way that people did in the past. While we know that miracles have not been proven, to Thomas they had been. Miracles were something that just happened and needed no further explanation. We don't need to know anything about theology or science at the time that he was writing to understand that this was a fact, we just need to look at the way that he expressed the information. He did not talk about something being a possibility, or a worry, or a concern, he talked about something being. While, clearly, it is not an absolute truth (what is?) it *was* for Thomas, a *fact*. Separating the author's understanding of what was factual and what was an opinion is important because it will very often differ from what you understand facts to be. This will be explored in more detail in the section on suspending disbelief.

IDENTIFYING AUTHORS IN COMPLEX TEXTS.

In every HAT exam to date, the author of the text has been identified to the candidates at the beginning, before they read the passage. While you might think this means that identifying the author is just a matter of working out their sphere or influences, you might be surprised how many candidates still make mistakes.

HAT examiners will sometimes choose texts which play tricks on you. The most common way of doing this with your understanding of authorship is through a dialogue. This was a style of writing common in ancient Greece and the European Renaissance, so there are plenty of opportunities to show up.

In a dialogue, the author writes down a conversation between multiple people, none of whom may be the author themselves, and uses the different personae involved in the conversation to explore a point of view from multiple perspectives. For example, you might have a HAT paper which looks something like this:

> *This is a passage taken from* La Villa Strangiato, *a philosophical text written by Sicilian renegade Nellus Paert, Methius and Thisbe were friends of his, residing at his villa, and he used them in his writing.*
>
> Thisbe: And what of the shepherds? Are they also, in spite of their strength, to wallow in the muck as poor savages purely by virtue of their occupation, by which they feed us and give us cloth? Are their pursuits less noble than ours?
>
> Methius: Indeed the life of the shepherds is a hard one, bound as they are to the earth, often without family or home, though to equate the nobility of their pursuits to a nobility of purpose and of life is to omit the greatest truth of our world; that the Almighty God has determined an order to the world which is so perfectly designed as to ensure we can coexist and pursue the greatest delights. Would you, yourself, be able to write and sing as you do were you forced to raise sheep from dawn until dusk, and watch them at night?

With papers like this, many candidates fall into the trap of talking about the contrasting opinions of Methius and Thisbe, and even make comments about what this can reveal about gender dynamics or friendship. It is important to remember that neither Methius nor Thisbe are real, so all they can reflect there, at most is the author's views on friendship or gender dynamics in their own writing. Both parts of the text are representative of Paert's own knowledge and views, he is the sole author of this text, and he is using both of these characters as an artistic device. While we know that both Methius and Thisbe were real people, they did not have the conversation that is being described here, we know instead that Paert used them as a literary tool.

Whenever you have a text like this, one of the most important survival tools is to remember that there is one author (unless you are *explicitly* told otherwise in the introductory text before the passage begins.) Whenever you talk about what the passage can reveal to you about the past, it is revealing a single point of view, and a single sphere. Revelations you may be able to draw from the interaction between fictional characters is limited by being fictional. That is not to say it is useless, you can draw a great deal of information from fictional texts because they reflect the author's non-fictional values, beliefs and ideas, but you must remember who the actual author is. Talking about Methius or Thisbe's opinion uncritically is a sure-fire way to pick up some low-level indicators and crash your final mark.

IDENTIFYING THE SUBJECTS OF A SOURCE

We've looked at a lot of material on who wrote the source. Something else that you need to consider when analysing sources, not just in the HAT but in university-level historical research, is the source's subject.

Fundamentally, this means learning how to identify who the source is talking about and determining whether and how this can shape your response.

The way that you identify the subjects of the source follows on from your reading of it, particularly your focus on the central theme(s), as much as they can exist. When you are given the passage, identify the central themes, the big message, and ask yourself "who is this telling me about?" This can be very specific, being about one individual (like the earlier source talking about Rasmus), or about the population of an entire town or even country.

If you are still stuck, a useful tip is to look for personal pronouns like 'her' 'his' 'they' 'their' 'I' etc, work out who the subject of those pronouns is. That person will be one of the subjects, if not the only subject.

As an example, let's return to an earlier example of a source from this guide.

> Her marriage celebration was greater than any other that had taken place at the palace, a celebration befitting the important status of her husband. He was famous everywhere in the country for having co-operated with the British when they first arrived in Katsina. At the time Muhammadu Dikko was not yet Emir but was known as a counsellor. Because of his success with the British colonial officers he was elevated to the status of Emir of Katsina. He saw to it that Ma'daki reached Katsina accompanied by her family's wealth; her slaves, her dowry, and her parents' gifts of grains and other foods – corn, millet, rice, wheat, palm oil, groundnut oil, butter, etc. – for her new in-laws. Everything was loaded onto horses and camels because at the time there were no cars. After she reached Katsina another wedding celebration was held and this one was even bigger than the one held in Kano. Some years after the wedding the Emir decided to take Ma'daki around the countryside to show her his domain. After that he decided to take her everywhere he went.

The first thing to do then is to identify the central themes. The passage is discussing the great wealth of Muhammadu Dikko and the considerable size of the marriage celebrations when he married Ma'daki. From this, we can infer that the subjects of the source are Muhammadu and Ma'daki. We can back this up by looking at the personal pronouns. 'Her' and 'she' exclusively refers to Ma'daki, while 'he' and 'his' exclusively refers to Muhammadu. This source then has two subjects.

Why does this matter? Because knowing the subjects allows you to check and refine your conclusions. You can talk about the information that you can learn about two people in particular, and use that as the foundation of your wider claims. For example:

"We can see that some people had higher status than others, and that some people were rich"

is a much worse demonstration of your analytical skill than:

"Through the description of Ma'daki, we can see that she experienced considerable wealth, and that this was a factor in her marrying someone of as high a status as Muhammadu. This tells us that the society in which they both lived was a socially stratified one, with political power and wealth both being markers of high-status, though there may be others."

Identifying the source can be a great way to ensure that, when you are planning out and writing your answer, you can write within the confines of what the source can actually tell you. It almost forces you to show your thinking, when you inevitably have to connect the subject to the wider contexts required for the answer, and that's a great trick.

TENSES

Tenses are one of the most frustrating survival essentials to include. For the vast majority of us it isn't something we particularly have to think about. We can communicate with people and be understood just fine.

In the HAT, however, you are writing a note for someone else to pick up and read later, when they do, you need to make sure that they have a really clear idea of what you are saying, and one of the most common mistakes and hindrances to clarity that we see as examiners is a poor use of tenses.

Understanding the basics of maintaining a constant tense, being aware of tense, can also be helpful for your analysis of the passage given to you in the HAT. This is because sometimes, the author's use of tenses can give you information that is otherwise hidden, and being aware of tense as you work will help you pick up on this. For example, a source in which the author says:

"We ran as fast as we could from the school all the way back to the church, knowing that it would take days to reach our home town on foot as no one in the village had a car (we have one now)."

Careful attention to their use of past and present tense tells us that the author is writing this some time after the events they are describing. The comment in brackets makes it clear that they have one now, in their present, but no one did at the time they are describing running to the church. Careful attention to whether the author is talking about the past or present can reveal useful information about the limitations of the source.

The future tense can also be incredibly important to spot. Let's look at an example here from a previous HAT exam.

> *I wrapped the book in the folds of my sigachima and returned to school. That night, my friends and I began our laborious task. But we kept on working, month after month. As soon as we finished a copy, we smuggled it out of the school grounds, and Pastor Kim helped us get it into the hands of patriotic young men and spiritual leaders who were forming secret study circles that would someday become centres of the resistance movement.*

The question was about what the source can reveal about society and culture in early twentieth-century Korea. Past candidates really struggled with this aspect of the source, and would often talk about the fact that the existence of a resistance movement can tell us that the occupying force in the country was strongly opposed and unpopular, as a resistance movement wouldn't exist without opposition to some dominant force, either an occupation or a despotic government. However, close attention to the tenses used by the author reveals that the resistance is being talked about here in the future tense, meaning that we don't know that a resistance movement existed in early twentieth-century Korea. This mistake cost several candidates their place at interview from otherwise great transcripts, and it's a minor error which can be solved by paying close attention to the tenses being used.

When it comes to writing your response though, there are two main things that you need to remember:

1) Always keep the author's actions, beliefs, and the things they describe in the past tense.
2) Ensure that you remain consistent in your use of tenses.

There have been countless instances in our experience as examiners when the student will talk about the fact that "the people lived in a society in which deaths by drowning were commonplace" in one sentence, and that "the author clearly thinks that these deaths are acceptable, and an example of God damning our world" in the next. It is, in the grand scheme of things, a minor issue, but your HAT response is not particularly long, and even minor issues can have a significant impact, as each mark moves you 2.5% toward or away from an interview.

INFERENCES FROM THE EXISTENCE OF THE SOURCE.

This is a really important survival essential, as it's a trick to thinking about source analysis in a way which is often not really taught at school, and will often produce some great high-level indicators.

The core principle is that, when you are examining the passage given to you in the HAT, and trying to determine what it can tell you about the past, people generally focus on what the source says. This isn't unreasonable, but in doing so they often completely ignore what the source can tell you from what it is, from the fact that it exists at all.

Let's look at a few examples:

> *This passage is taken from a text written and published by a Roman slaveowner and magistrate, following a successful slave uprising in 302AD, in which he describes his capture, torture, and imprisonment.*

So, in this example, we know that the magistrate is going to be talking about the awful things happening to him, he has been captured, tortured, and imprisoned after his slaves have risen up against him. Candidates with this question will often claim that this shows us society at the time is in a state of flux, with slaves throwing off the chains of their masters.

While this is partially true, we can also say something else, based purely on the fact that you are reading the passage at all. The magistrate survived to write his account and survived long enough for his account to be published. This means that while he was probably captured, tortured, and imprisoned, he wasn't killed, and more importantly, he seems to have still been a slave owner at the point that his account was released. The existence of the source tells us that while the uprising may have been successful, pre-existing power structures may have been partially or fully restored shortly thereafter, and society valued this person's account sufficiently highly for it to be preserved for over 1700 years.

> *This passage is taken from a text written by Gregory, a bishop in Tours, a city ruled by Clovis's successors. He chronicles events from nine decades previously.*

This one is a little different. In this example candidates often made some really great points about Clovis, who he was, and what he did, and what this could tell them about being king.

We know, though, more than that. From the existence of this source we can determine that Clovis and his descendants were interested in his deeds, and his virtue in the eyes of the Christian God. That a religious figure recorded this nine decades after the fact also tells us that the source is part of a history and that the recording of past events for posterity was something which was clearly valued in the society of the time, and senior figures in society were appointed to create such texts.

> *This passage is taken from a text written by Toby, a user of online bulletin boards in 1996. He decries the passage of a new law which makes it illegal to criticise the United States' government in online communications.*

In this final example, candidates can use this passage to talk about the fact that the American government was restricting communications, and actively prevented people from freely expressing their opinions concerning the business of government. While this is true, it would be very easy for candidates to argue that this means that internet society of the period was restricted, and following earlier criticism, the government had created a law managing online spaces which prevented them being criticised.

Hopefully, by this stage, you can see where this is going. The source itself is an online post criticising the American government. Its existence is proof that such criticisms not only continued but were widely distributed and preserved historically. This can also tell you that the law managing online communications was not only widely criticised after its release, but the law itself failed to serve as an effective deterrent.

The important thing to remember then is to always consider what conclusions, if any, you can draw from the fact that the source you are reading was created, preserved, and placed in the exam paper you are working on.

LEARNING FROM THE AUTHOR'S ASSUMPTIONS

A common problem which students come across in the HAT is passages that, on the surface, appear to be unreliable. This can be because they are showing a clearly heavily biased viewpoint, or because they are reporting on something which happened a long time ago. Identifying these kinds of limitations has already been covered, as have some of the ways in which you can draw information from them, however, these kinds of inferences are a vital component of high-level source analysis, which is what the examiners are looking for.

Let's take our first example, a source with a heavily biased viewpoint. If the author of the source is someone who you believe to be strongly influenced by a particular ideology or inclined to either condemn or defend the subject of their writing, then it can be very easy to claim that the source is unreliable, or otherwise unusable or unsuitable for the HAT because the author cannot be trusted to give an honest opinion. However, the truth is far from it, and that is because if the author's own biases and prejudices rendered the source unreliable or limited its value, then that would be an issue for every single source used in the HAT. In fact, the value comes from what the source can tell you about the author's biases.

A classic instance of this is a Nazi Germany source. An example is given below:

This is the transcript of an interview between Rudolf Schenitzer and James Lafferty in 1954. Schenitzer had been a Nazi party member until 1944 and after the war moved to the countryside where he worked as a school teacher. Here, he has been asked what people's reasons were for joining the Nazi party in 1936.

"For years Germany had been betrayed by succession after succession of corrupt leaders. Degeneracy had taken root in the fatherland and it was clear to many of us that drastic change was needed. For some of us, I think the change was more drastic than they felt it could have been, but nonetheless, it was needed. Hitler was the only way to make that change happen, the best way. We all believed that he would be able to reduce the rampant corruption and abuses that had abounded before. The way we were treated after [the first world war] was absolutely barbaric and was designed to kill off the entire German race. If we had not joined Hitler, and fought for the settlement we eventually secured with [the allies] we would not be speaking now, we would be dead, all the German race would be dead, and you would instead be talking with some Jew, or harlot. Hitler has only been made out to be a poor leader because he, himself, was also betrayed, and the victors make the history, even if it is false. I and many men like me believed, and still believe, that national socialism is the only way to protect Germany, protect our way of life, protect our economy. It is a shame that our liberties have been so restricted after the war that we can no longer publicly speak the truth, but it is better to know the truth in your heart and be a proud aryan than a deceitful degenerate sympathiser."

What can this extract tell you about politics and society in 1930s Germany?

Students often struggle with sources like this because they can recognise clearly that the author is saying things which are wrong, he is heavily biased and is seeking to justify his position and defend himself, and so his opinion is not a good indicator of politics and society in 1930s Germany.

However, in those cases, they're all dead wrong. This is a *fantastic* source because it tells you so much about what people who joined the Nazi party believed. You don't have to think they are right, even for a moment, to recognise that you are being given detailed insight into the thinking and propaganda of the Nazi political machine and the nature of the discourse which abounded at the time. There is a great deal that can actually be made of this source.

In order to pick up on this, a good HAT candidate has to stay aware of the fact that what the author is describing is only one component of what the source can tell you, among many. The source's existence, and the ways in which the author thinks, based on the way they describe things, can be great sources of information, and in questions like this would be your *primary* source of information!

FICTION

While one kind of 'unreliable' source lambasted by candidates is the one clearly marred by bias, another that comes up is fiction. We've mentioned a few times already in the guide that fiction can be just as useful as non-fiction to the historian, but a note here on how it is useful can really help candidates struggling to grasp how something *literally made up* could tell them anything real about the past.

A number of different fictional texts have been used in past HAT papers, we have an example below from a work of fiction. Read it and see if you can determine what, if anything, we can learn about the culture and society which produced it.

This is a passage from Homer's Odyssey, composed around 800 BCE.

Every one was speechless with surprise at seeing a man there, but Ulysses began at once with his petition.

"Queen Arete," he exclaimed, "daughter of great Rhexenor, in my distress I humbly pray you, as also your husband and these your guests (whom may heaven prosper with long life and happiness, and may they leave their possessions to their children, and all the honours conferred upon them by the state) to help me home to my own country as soon as possible; for I have been long in trouble and away from my friends."

Then he sat down on the hearth among the ashes and they all held their peace, till presently the old hero Echeneus, who was an excellent speaker and an elder among the Phaeacians, plainly and in all honesty addressed them thus:

"Alcinous," said he, "it is not creditable to you that a stranger should be seen sitting among the ashes of your hearth; every one is waiting to hear what you are about to say; tell him, then, to rise and take a seat on a stool inlaid with silver, and bid your servants mix some wine and water that we may make a drink offering to Jove the lord of thunder, who takes all well disposed suppliants under his protection; and let the housekeeper give him some supper, of whatever there may be in the house."

When Alcinous heard this he took Ulysses by the hand, raised him from the hearth, and bade him take the seat of Laodamas, who had been sitting beside him, and was his favourite son. A maid servant then brought him water in a beautiful golden ewer and poured it into a silver basin for him to wash his hands, and she drew a clean table beside him; an upper servant brought him bread and offered him many good things of what there was in the house, and Ulysses ate and drank. Then Alcinous said to one of the servants, "Pontonous, mix a cup of wine and hand it round that we may make drink-offerings to Jove the lord of thunder, who is the protector of all well-disposed suppliants."

Even though this is a work of fiction, there is, in fact, quite a lot that we can learn here. None of the events have to be real for us to know that the author placed considerable value on treating guests well. We can also see that the treatment of guests is something supervised by a deity, Jove, and so we can say that this was a culture in which notions of a god, or gods existed, and therefore it was likely they had some form of religion. Mention of 'heaven' also suggests that this is a culture familiar with the concept of an afterlife.

> *"**Queen** Arete," he exclaimed, "daughter of great Rhexenor, in my distress I humbly pray you, as also your husband and these your guests (whom may **heaven prosper** with long life and happiness, and may they **leave their possessions to their children**, and all the honours conferred upon them by **the state**) to help me home to **my own country** as soon as possible; for I have been long in trouble and away from my friends."*
>
> *Then he sat down on the hearth among the ashes and they all held their peace, till presently the old hero Echeneus, who was an excellent speaker and an elder among the Phaeacians, plainly and in all honesty addressed them thus:*

We can also tell that this was a society in which monarchies were not unusual. The queen is introduced without any elaboration on her role or the root of her power. We can also see that the author is describing a system of familial inheritance and a state. While we don't know that these existed in the author's own world, we can certainly argue that it is likely. Similarly, we know that the author was aware of the concept of countries, and the combination of this with states can tell us that theirs was a society in which they existed within a nation-state, which in one way or another interacted with other nation-states.

> *"Alcinous," said he, "it is not creditable to you that a stranger should be seen sitting among the ashes of your hearth; every one is waiting to hear what you are about to say; tell him, then, to rise and take a seat on a stool inlaid with silver, and bid your **servants** mix some wine and water that we may make a drink offering to **Jove the lord of thunder**, who takes all well disposed suppliants under his protection; and let **the housekeeper** give him some supper, of whatever there may be in the house."*
>
> *When Alcinous heard this he took Ulysses by the hand, raised him from the hearth, and bade him take the seat of Laodamas, who had been sitting beside him, and was his favourite son. A **maid servant** then brought him water in a beautiful golden ewer and poured it into a silver basin for him to wash his hands, and she drew a clean table beside him; an **upper servant** brought him bread and offered him many good things of what there was in the house, and Ulysses ate and drank. Then Alcinous said to one of the servants, "Pontonous, mix a cup of wine and hand it round that we may make drink-offerings to **Jove the lord of thunder, who is the protector of all well-disposed suppliants."***

Furthermore, we also have mention of housekeepers and servants, we can't say that people routinely had these in the author's world (this is, after all, the house of a queen) but we can tell that their society had a division of labour, with different people filling different roles, and implications of a socially stratified culture. An allusion to maidservants and upper servants further reinforces the notion that there are different ranks within servants in the society of the author's intended audience, as these notes are presented without further comment.

All of these points, of course, can be elaborated further in your response to the HAT, but it is clear that there is a tremendous amount of information that we can learn here.

LEARNING FROM THE AUTHOR'S NORMALISATIONS

One of the most valuable skills to use in analysing fiction, as well as in any other source, is to pay attention to details which the author mentions, but doesn't discuss in any detail. For instance, mentioning a man 'drawing his sword' or 'asking his slaves to leave him be' not only tells you that carrying swords was common, or keeping slaves for that matter, but also that they were sufficiently commonplace to not merit further discussion. They weren't notable, and that in and of itself is of note to you, as the historian, because again it gives you insight into the values, assumptions, and sphere of the author, and you need all of that information to be able to build the most accurate picture possible of the past. The exact wording of your question will vary in the HAT, but that's the basis of what every test is about; creating an accurate and detailed interpretation of the past based on a single source.

Another example of this comes from a source we have looked at previously, about Clovis and his rise to power:

> While Clovis[1] was in Paris, he sent secretly to Chloderic, the son of Sigibert[2], saying 'Your father is old. If he were to die, his kingdom would come to you of right and my alliance would come with it.' Chloderic was led astray by his lust for power and began to plot his father's death. He set assassins on him and had him murdered, so that he might gain possession of his kingdom. By the judgement of God, Chloderic fell into the same pit that he had dug for his father. He sent messengers to King Clovis to announce his father's death. 'My father is dead,' said he, 'and I have taken over his kingdom and his treasure. Send me your envoys and I will gladly hand over to you anything that you may care to select from this treasure.' 'I thank you for your good will,' answered Clovis. 'I ask you to show all your treasure to my messengers, but you may keep it …' [The envoys came, saw the treasure and encouraged Chloderic to finger the gold in a chest] As he leaned forward to do this, one of the Franks raised his double-headed axe and split Chloderic's skull. This unworthy son thus shared the fate of his father. When Clovis heard that both were dead, he came to Cologne himself and ordered the inhabitants to assemble. 'Chloderic, the son of your King, my brother, was plotting against his father and putting it out that I wanted him killed. As Sigibert fled, Chloderic had him murdered. While Chloderic was showing his father's treasure, he in turn was killed by somebody or other. I take no responsibility for what has happened. It is not for me to shed the blood of one of my fellow kings, for that is a crime. But since things have turned out this way, you should turn to me and put yourselves under my protection.' The men of Cologne clashed their shields and shouted their approval; they raised Clovis on a shield and made him their ruler. Thus he took over both the kingship and the treasure and submitted Sigibert's people to his own rule. Day in day out God submitted the enemies of Clovis to his dominion and increased his power, for he walked before him with an upright heart and did what was pleasing in his sight.

---

[1] A Frankish king, based in Paris, and recently converted to Christianity
[2] King of the Franks in modern Germany

The question asks candidates to see what they can learn about being king at the time. Candidates often identify that it was bloody, and involved a degree of manipulation, plotting and deception. There are several examples here of minor details mentioned by the author which you can also pick up on.

For example, the author mentions Chloderic saying "I have taken over his kingdom and his treasure" the treasure is mentioned again, later, as part of the cause of Chloderic's death. What candidates often miss is that as well as Chloderic inheriting his father's kingdom, treasure (which was literally a chest of gold) was also something which passed from king to king, and having access to such treasure was a fundamental part of kingship.

Similarly, the single mention of a 'double-headed' axe tells us that the people in the company of kings were often heavily armed, and this can tell us about the experiences of kings at the time. Similarly, near the end of the passage, Clovis is acclaimed by the population by clashing their shields together and raising him on them to proclaim him their ruler. The author doesn't explain this in any further detail, but that tells us a couple of things. Firstly, it tells us that when there is a transition of power, anyone seeking to become king must secure the approval of the population. Secondly, we know those who turn out to hear the prospective king's case do so armed. Finally, we can also determine that kingship is determined, at least partially, by military strength and prowess.

ASSUMPTIONS FROM THE CONTENT OF THE SOURCE.

Sometimes, the HAT passage does not have a clear author. You cannot identify a central theme, a sphere, an audience or even a subject. Sources can be entirely descriptive, and the extent to which you can use the author as a determinant of civilisation or culture is very limited. There is, obviously, always an author there, but they can be very hard to see.

In this case, what you have to do is focus on what is being described. We've previously said that you should not only focus on the description, but what goes around it, and this is true, but it isn't always possible. In these kinds of cases, you only have two real sources of information: the material described in the source, and the existence of the source.

If you focus on the description, you can use similar techniques to those outlined above, when learning from the author's normalisations; focus on what is mentioned without further comment, and see what that can tell you about what's normal, what's common, and go from there.

This can be a very tricky area to prepare for, but it has come up in the HAT before and could do again. To that end, we are going to look at the text from an actual HAT past paper which did this (HAT 2013). We generally have tried to avoid using actual past papers so that you can have as many fresh ones to practice with as possible, but this was such a great example we felt it could be really valuable to give you a walk-through for this challenging paper.

This passage is taken from an inventory of objects taken out of a house owned and used by Catholic missionaries in Baghdad, following a raid on the house by officials from the Ottoman Empire in the year 1701. Baghdad was under Ottoman control at the time, and the population was mostly Muslim, with minority Christian and Jewish groups. This inventory was created by one of the missionaries, who sent it back to their headquarters in France. You don't need to know anything about Iraq in the 18th century AD.

1. A large chiming clock.
2. 8 watches of which six were left by deceased clerics in Baghdad, and two others deposited by merchants in exchange for 110 *piastres*.[1]
3. 2 large baskets filled with porcelain objects including two vases of great value.
4. 2 cases filled with surgical, medical, and mathematical instruments.
5. Books belonging to the two libraries of the household in Mosul, all of which had been transported to Baghdad when that mission was razed to the ground.
6. Provisions consisting of 150 *okas*[2] of oil; 40 *okas* of butter; more than 400 bushels of wheat; 150 *okas* of rice; 12 *okas* of pepper; 6 *okas* of cinnamon; 3 pounds of cloves; and 600 kernels of nutmeg.
7. An assortment of cooking utensils and crockery, many of which had been left by the people of this country as well as 'Franks'[3] passing through on their way back from India or Persia who preferred not to carry them across the desert.
8. Furniture for 5 or 6 rooms for use by travelling Franks who have nowhere else to stay but with the Fathers.
9. Instruments for the apothecary including basins and heaters for the baths, a bowl of ambergris[4], and other items necessary for the making of remedies.
10. 3 chests decorated in the Turkish fashion full of all sorts of precious remedies.
11. A few coins for daily expenses, no more than 20 or 30 *piastres*.
12. 6 good pieces of golden and silver fabric from the Indies donated for the decoration of the church.
13. A bundle of very fine cloth of this country, embroidered in gold, about 40 pieces.
14. A large chest full of very fine 'Indian', basic muslin, and some cotton fabric.
15. A large silver chalice[5] that we no longer use.
16. A considerable number of pearls, coral, and amber.
17. 11 medium-sized Turkish carpets, and 3 Persian carpets for use in the church.
18. 2 large paintings, about 15 feet high: one of the Virgin Mary and the other of King Louis XIV sent from Paris by the directors of the East India Company, along with two more of the same paintings in a medium size.
19. 6 large candles in the style of this country, each weighing 5 *okas*.
20. A provision of wax for the church, about 80 *okas*.
21. 6 large magnifying glasses left by those Fathers who passed away in this house.

---

[1] French currency
[2] Ottoman unit of measurement, about 1.3 kg
[3] Europeans living in the Ottoman Empire
[4] A waxy substance used in perfumes and medicines of the time
[5] A goblet used in Catholic religious ceremonies

22. A rifle and two pistols given by Mr Caré upon his return from India, where he had been sent by King Louis XIV.
23. A Turkish sword given by a priest, Fr Beauvilliers.

What does this passage tell us about the lives of missionaries living in Iraq in the 17th and 18th centuries?

Take a moment to read this source and review it in the context of the question. If you have been able to keep up with the techniques already covered, you should be able to learn a lot from this source already. If you've never seen anything like this before though, it can be challenging. Don't worry, we'll cover what information you can pull from this source, and importantly how we did it!

One thing we know is that religious people, who may not be the same people as the missionaries, left their belongings to the missionaries when they died. This tells us that, at the very least, there was a religious community in which the missionaries existed, and for one reason or another, a lot of them die. This can either tell us that they have been there for a long time, or that being a religious figure in Iraq at the time was quite dangerous. If we add to this information item 21, the magnifying glasses left by Fathers who passed away in the house, it's safe to assume that the missionaries have been operating there for a long time, and when they die many of them leave possessions to the other missionaries. Based on the raid, and what happened in Mosul (point 5) it was also, it seems, quite dangerous.

We can also see from point one that the missionaries in Iraq were operating as loan providers to merchants. We have a description here of watches deposited by merchants in exchange for capital, in other words, collateral. Items 2, 6, 13, and 16 might also suggest that the house was being used to store items for merchants or others, as we know they are storing books which are not their own from item 5, and it is hard to imagine a single house, occupied by people able to trade with locals (proven in item 11) requiring nearly 200 kilos of oil! Many of the other items, particularly items 3, 13, and 16 seem to have no connection to the missionaries themselves, and the best explanation is that they are either being used in the same way as the watches, or are being stored there. There is certainly, as a result, the implication that the missionaries did not feel that the house was in serious danger of attack or raid, by virtue of keeping so many items of great value there (3, 10, 13, 15, 16). This tells us that the missionaries in Iraq were involved with local business, and were not particularly isolated from the society in which they lived.

While it may seem as though the missionaries are wealthy, as they retain many objects of considerable value, we know that some of these, such as items 7, 12, and 18 were gifts, and that the money they had for their own daily expenses was around 20% the value of a single watch, from items 1 and 11. So the point we can get from this is that the missionaries did not have much disposable income, but were based at a house filled with valuable items. The conclusion you can draw from this is that many of these items did not belong to them, and either belonged to the organisation they worked for or to people who were merely storing those items in their house, perhaps for a fee. That they were able to use french currency for daily expenses in Baghdad tells us that piastres were accepted and used locally, reinforcing the assumption that the merchants mentioned are more likely to be local.

The notion that the missionaries did work in the Iraqi community can be further supported by item 9, which detailed a range of instruments for the manufacturing of medicines. Either the missionaries got sick a lot, or they were treating the sick in Iraq. This is further supported by item 4, which mentions surgical and medical instruments, and item 10 (arguably, the fine muslin in point 14, as both fine and non-ornamental, was for use in wound dressings). Either they were storing supplies for medical treatment, or they were practicing basic medical care themselves. As point 9 implies that the house had its own baths (plural) it could be argued that the medical care was taking place in the missionaries house, and therefore they were carrying it out.

The books in item 5 are also important because they came from another missionary house in somewhere called Mosul, and that that house had been razed. From this, we can make two observations about the lives of missionaries; first that there are other missionaries operating outside of Baghdad, and there is a wider community for them to interact with. Second, is that there is clearly some hostility towards missionaries in Iraq. One house was torn down, another has been raided by authorities and many possessions seized.

Item 7 shows us that both Europeans and Iraqis 'passed through' the house. It was being used by the local community and travellers from Europe. This tells us that the missionaries lives were at least partially integrated with the local population and that they often encountered other people from Europe who were not missionaries. They were not alone as Europeans in Iraq. What's more, as the other Franks had 'nowhere else to stay' but with the mission (point 9), there's a much more intricate point to be made about their role in Baghdad. We know from points 7, 22, and 23 that Europeans were stopping at the house specifically on their return from actions further East. We know that at least one of these Europeans was sent directly by King Louis XIV, and his ties to the East India Company in Paris (shown by point 18) imply that he was a French king, and so it is reasonable to assume that agents of the French state are stopping at the house, on their return to Europe, and that it is the only safe place for them to stay in Baghdad prior to their return to Europe. When we consider that all of these returning Franks left items in the care of the missionaries – there's a further point that we can make: the rest of the journey West, to Europe, was less dangerous: they no longer needed these items, so this house marked a boundary point at which it became less safe for Europeans travelling East (none of them left items there while travelling out, only back, as far as we can tell). These missionaries were, therefore, functioning as a 'safehouse' for travelling agents of the French state, and from the gifts sent by the East India Company in Paris, we can round this out by inferring that they were not solely in Baghdad as missionaries of Catholicism, but themselves agents of French interests in Persia, Turkey, and the Indies. When we then consider that the church was seemingly left out of the raid, it raises questions about the *cause* of the raid – was it because Christianity was a minority religion, or was it that these missionaries were providing services beyond proselytizing?

We also know from item 12 that the missionaries had access to a church, which they were expected to decorate and maintain, for which they received a number of donations and valuable items from France, also evidenced by items 17, 18, and 20. This also means that we can say that the missionaries were actively participating in religious duties, as Christians, in Iraq, and that they were able to maintain a church for a minority religion at the time. Item 15, however, suggests that religious practice may have waned in some way if the chalice is no longer being used, or that the chalice has been replaced by a new one, kept in the church, and not targeted by the raid. The latter seems more likely, as the considerable amount of wax kept for church candles would be otherwise unnecessary.

The descriptions of a range of items, as Turkish, Persian, Indian, or from the Indies, suggests that the house contained a number of high-value items and that a point of significance was their origin outside of Iraq. There may well be a confirmation bias here, of the Ottomans were focusing on confiscating items of value, though this cannot be confirmed. We can say that the missionaries living in Iraq had access to a large number of items from a range of locations throughout Eurasia. Similarly, item 18 shows us that items were being sent to the missionaries from Europe, and these were not just based on survival, but luxury items like paintings. From this, we can infer that the missionaries were established and relatively comfortable if the East India Company could send them luxury goods safely.

The only things specifically described as being Iraqi are items 7, 13, and 19, and even then, the candles are only in 'the style of this country', from this we can infer that the missionaries interacted with the people of Iraq, but perhaps not very much with Iraqi goods unless, as mentioned above, the Ottomans were not interested in confiscating Iraqi goods.

Items 22 and 23 also suggest that those returning to Europe were not only safe from there out, but they felt that the missionaries may have greater use for weaponry in Baghdad. We know that the sword was important, as was the name of the person who gave it to them, and that the Ottomans seized it. From these points, we can infer that the missionaries also served as hosts to priests on missions outside of Iraq and that they provided some kind of service for doing so, in which valuable and potentially useful items were gifted to them.

As you can see, there is a lot we can tell about the lives of missionaries in Iraq at the time, even though, in this source, we have no clear author, audience, central theme or sphere. We can, however, examine each point in the source and consider "what can I imagine their world looking like based on this?" Put yourself in the shoes of a contemporary reader, and imagine the whole thing makes sense, seems normal. What assumptions do you have to make in order for the source to make sense to you?

If you can draw conclusions like this from these sources, there aren't any source types left that can flummox you. That means that we can get on to some of the survival essentials for saving yourself from common source analysis mistakes.

HOW TO SUSPEND YOUR DISBELIEF

We have previously made mention of sources that contain elements which we know, fundamentally, to be untrue, whether they are detailed descriptions of miracles, magic, or people with the heads of dogs. What you have to do, as the candidate sitting the HAT exam, is remember that the examiners have chosen the passage to test you, and they wouldn't include things which were not useful to you.

In the previous section, we mentioned putting yourself in the shoes of a contemporary reader. That is also really useful in suspending your disbelief as well, in being able to read a text, and respond to things which you know, personally, are not true, or not relevant. Remember that you can't bring in your own knowledge, and wherever possible this means that when things in the source *conflict* with that knowledge, you need to force yourself to pretend that they are true and ask yourself what that *means* for the people living when this source was created!

Suspending your disbelief does not mean the same thing as repeating the material described in the source as the truth. If that were the case, every HAT would be dead easy; just repeat what the author says in your own words. Instead, what you have to do is learn to analyse what is being said by the author, without writing off the things that you know are mistaken as irrelevant. If the author talks about the townsfolk being cursed by a wizard to fall victim to a terrible plague, you know that they saw disease as being caused by magic, lived in a world where magic was a believable cause for things, and that there were individuals identified by society as wizards. If you read the sentence and decide that, because obviously it wasn't because of a wizard, we can't tell what really happened, you're missing the point.

If you come across a passage in the HAT which contains material like this, which is not uncommon, just remember; the author believed all of this to be true. You don't have to, but you need to have at the forefront of your analysis that in the author's time, and society, this was all perfectly believable. You can use that to determine what kinds of beliefs, social structures, superstitions etc there were. It can also be used to tell you about the extent of the author's sphere, and how they handled things outside of it. Is the default for things beyond your own sphere, in the context you are examining, to assume the work of magic or a god? If you can suspend your disbelief, and think like the author, then you are on your way to recognising the fundamental elements of the author's society which may be so different from your own.

Recognising, explaining, and evidencing these differences is a significant part of the HAT, and if you can successfully analyse your source in this way, place yourself in the mindset of the author, you'll be well on your way to creating a great response. What you have to do, though, is take your inferences, your thoughts, and your notes, and convert those into a great plan, so that you know just what to write.

HAT SURVIVAL ESSENTIALS – ESSAY PLANNING

After you have analysed the source and made notes from it, highlighting the relevant material as we've shown you in this guide, the next most important thing is planning out your answer. This is, actually, more important than the writing stage. Obviously, you have to write an answer to get a mark, but how good your answer is, will be based largely on how well you plan it.

In the plan, what you want to do is take all of the notes you made while reading the source and organise them into a rough structure. The exact structure you use will vary depending on the passage you have been given and the question, but you will want to create a plan regardless, and we will show you how you can use the examiner's requirements and your approximation of the mark scheme to create that plan in a moment.

When you are planning your essay though, there are some really important tips that we would like to stress:

Answer the question

- This may seem obvious, but in your plan, before you start writing, make sure that you have a clear answer to the question. You can put this at the very top of your plan, as you'll want to mention it at the start of your essay, and refer back to it as you go.

Collect your ideas

- The first thing you have to do is take the ideas you have in your notes, and ensure that you take the ones which you think are the most important, and have them all mentioned somewhere in your main plan.

Check your narrative

- Once you have all of the points assembled, they will form the backbone of your answer. You need to make sure that all of your points flow logically from one to the other and, crucially, that they all contribute towards your own answer to the question, and don't contradict your own argument.

Make notes of your main evidence

- In your plan, when you've arranged your points to follow the narrative, it is a good idea to make links to the specific parts of the passage which evidence each point, so that when you are writing you only need to look at your plan to know what your supporting evidence is.

In total, you want to spend about ten minutes pulling all your points together into a plan, checking that the plan makes sense, checking you can answer the question, and linking the best evidence you want to use to each of the points you plan to make. You must ensure that you address every single aspect of the question at this point, when you are making your plan, and before you start writing.

The most important thing when writing your essay is not changing direction halfway through. When you start writing, you shouldn't stop writing until you have finished producing a couple of sides of A4 on the subject. Knowing just what your answer is, and how you are backing it up before you begin means that you never have to stop to think.

HOW TO USE YOUR VERSION OF THE MARK SCHEME TO CREATE A PLAN.

Way back on page 26 we covered how to use the question to find the mark scheme. The question:

"What does this passage tell us about the political and cultural values of the author?"

gives us the 'mark scheme':

- Define 'political'
- Define 'cultural'
- Define 'values'
- Make unambiguous points about the political values of the author
- Make unambiguous points about the cultural values of the author
- Provide evidence for each of those points from the passage
- Focus exclusively on the author's own values
- Reach a definitive conclusion about the authors political and cultural values
- Ensure that these are organised into a piece of writing which makes sense

From this, we need to come up with a plan. Your definitions will always go in your first paragraph. You don't *need* a detailed introduction in the HAT, but establishing your answer, approach, and definitions will make it easier for the person marking your exam to understand what you are saying and where you are going with it, which also means that it is easier for them to give you higher marks.

That means that definitions go in paragraph 1. As for the points about the political and cultural values of the author, and backing those up, your mark scheme cannot just be turned into a plan. You need to rearrange these to make sense. In this example, from your notes, you'll want to identify points about the author's political and cultural values and arrange them. If some points work together, then you can combine them into a single paragraph, if not, break them out into smaller paragraphs. There is no limit, or indeed recommendation that we will give, for the number of paragraphs that you should write in the HAT, beyond the fact that more is better. A page of text is hard for examiners to read.

This means that you want a paragraph for each individual point about either their political values, their cultural values, or points which you can make that touch on both at once. In each of those paragraphs, you want to also include evidence supporting those particular points.

Once you have created a list of all the paragraphs you are going to make and linked those to the evidence you are going to include, make a note to include a concluding paragraph, and plan out what you are going to say. In your conclusion, you just want to reinforce (not restate) the points you have made. Your main point with the conclusion is to reinforce what you have already said, you do not want to add in new ideas, and you certainly don't want to change your answer. You want, instead, to draw together all the points you've made into a single statement which says the same thing without using the same evidence. A great conclusion, then, might say something like.

"Overall, the source gives us a glimpse into the mind of an author for whom magic is commonplace, and personal agency has been entirely abandoned in the name of divine providence. Predominantly, what this passage shows us is that Anarchy is the dominant political system they strive for, and as a result, their cultural identity is a fractured mix of influences and heritage from the community they have built for themselves."

This would include no new information and instead is just reinforcing your existing points *without* repeating yourself. This is a challenging skill to master, but good conclusions can help shape the lasting impression the examiner forms of your work.

To give you an idea of how to put this into practice, here is a specimen essay plan based on the question above.

Paragraph one
- Define cultural
- Define political
- Define values
- Answer the question

Paragraph two
- First point about political or social values of the author
- Supporting evidence from the passage for this point
- Explain which of the authors values this shows, with a link to the second point

Paragraph three
- Second point about political or social values of the author
- Supporting evidence from the passage for this point
- Explain which of the authors values this shows

Paragraph four
- Link to the second point with a third point about political or social values of the author
- Supporting evidence from the passage for this point
- Explain which of the authors values this shows with a link to the fourth point

Paragraph five
- Fourth point about political or social values of the author
- Supporting evidence from the passage for this point
- Explain which of the authors values this shows

Paragraph six
- Conclude by reinforcing existing points
- Answer the question again

NARRATIVE FLOW AND MAKING LINKS

There are several different ways that you can make essays flow, and hopefully this is something that you have worked on at school previously. However, as it is important that your HAT essay flows (writing consistently is an assessed component) we will cover some tips for narrative flow here.

One of the most important steps is to write as a reader. While you are planning out your essay, consider what it would be like for you to read this from scratch. Does your argument naturally follow from what you've already said? In other words, if you stop and read the plan back to yourself, does it make sense?

While planning, try to make sure you organise your points into a logical order so that the connections between points make sense. In the HAT, that means trying to identify themes which may be shared between points. You can emphasise these themes by writing topic sentences at the start of each paragraph, introduce your main point each time, and demonstrate how this connects to what you have already written.

A useful tip for this is to make use of transitional words or phrases which demonstrate how two of your points link together, things like "as a result", "therefore", "despite this" can help show the reader that there is a link to be made here. Make sure though that you have considered what these links are, by putting yourself in a reader's shoes and being logical. If you say "The king murdered his subjects in cold blood. As a result, he can be seen as a beneficent leader" it will just look like you don't know what you're saying.

Ensure in each of your paragraphs that you use the language of the question when demonstrating your answer. This can help create a common theme in your writing, and help the examiner see that all of your points are contributing towards a shared thread.

HAT SURVIVAL ESSENTIALS – ESSAY WRITING
USING EVIDENCE TO SUPPORT YOUR CLAIMS

A HAT essay must be persuasive. You have not only got to make points about the past, from the extract, but convince the examiner that you are right. In order to do that you have to identify a *range* of suitable points in order to support your claim. Sometimes, there will only be one piece of evidence to support a point, but in that case, the point you are making should be a minor one and linked to a larger point that you can support more fully in your essay.

By providing evidence to back up your points, and examples of whether those things are demonstrated in the text, you can show the examiner just how you have extracted an interpretation of the past from the material. This isn't just important in terms of persuasiveness to the examiner, it will also serve to demonstrate that you have good academic writing skills; you can cite evidence for your claims, and use those to demonstrate that the claims you have made are visible in the world that you can see in the passage.

The HAT is not a test of your own knowledge, but of your aptitude at source analysis and historical research. That means that, when you are providing evidence to support your claims, you must not, under any circumstances, use information which is not mentioned in the source, or in the notes which the examiners give you in the HAT. We've said it before, but it is worth reiterating that this will **reduce** your final mark. Do not, under any circumstances do it. If you want to make a point about the past, based on the extract, but you are not sure if your own knowledge is getting in the way, a quick test is to ask yourself "where in the paper can I find proof for this?" If you cannot find proof for it, it is from your own knowledge, and you shouldn't include that point.

Similarly, though it may seem obvious if you are planning to make a point but you do not have evidence to support it, don't make the point.

What you *should* do is make use of the information you are given in the exam to say as much as you can about the factor(s) they want you to discuss in the relevant time period. You need to show your resourcefulness, the amount of information you are able to extract, and you can only do this by clearly linking the points you are making to the question.

The next most important thing to bear in mind, with using evidence, is that it is not enough to simply place evidence in there, you must also **explain** very clearly why that evidence is relevant to your answer, *how* does that evidence back up your claim? If you can show that, then it can really reinforce your point!

Let's give you an example to demonstrate this, with a question and mock answer, see if you can find areas where the candidate should make more use of evidence:

The following extract, written after the defeat of Japan in 1945, recalls a girl's experience at a school in Korea in the early twentieth century.

You are not expected to know anything about Korea or the period. You must read carefully and critically, and use your skills of historical analysis to interpret the extract.

One day we demanded that our teachers give us courses in Korean history. When they refused, I called three of my closest friends. "Let us find a Korean history book and each night copy a few pages. It will be slow work, but in time we each will have in our possession the treasured story of our nation." I went alone to Pastor Kim's house and told him what I wanted to do.

He looked at me for a few minutes and then smiled. "You are really determined to save Korea, aren't you? I will take a chance. But remember, you are taking a chance too. If the Japanese should ever find you with this book in your possession, they will chop off your head."

I told him I was not frightened, but I was, and he knew it. Nevertheless, he went to a secret hiding place and took out a beautiful leather-bound book on which were written the words Dongkook Yuksa. Translated literally, this means "Oriental History." But the book was written by Korean historians writing mainly about our country. He handed the book to me, saying, "Here is your heritage. Love it. Cherish it. Protect it."

I wrapped the book in the folds of my sigachima and returned to school. That night, my friends and I began our laborious task. But we kept on working, month after month. As soon as we finished a copy, we smuggled it out of the school grounds, and Pastor Kim helped us get it into the hands of patriotic young men and spiritual leaders who were forming secret study circles that would someday become centres of the resistance movement.

One morning, Miss Golden and a few of the teachers came to our class. Their faces were white. Miss Golden spoke, but did not look at us. "Girls, something is happening here that is not good for the school or for any of us. If I do not tell the Japanese police about it, and they find out by themselves, this school will be closed and all of you will be jailed, possibly beaten, perhaps even killed. You all know to what I am referring."

What does this extract tell us about society and culture in early twentieth-century Korea?

Candidate response:

The source describes a girl's experiences at a school in Korea during the early half of the twentieth century. The source is written in the first-person past tense, thus implying that the events described in the source are the personal memories of the author. This autobiographical account can reveal a lot of Korean society and culture during this period. For example, the source describes themes of occupation and repression, the role which history and tradition played in society, childhood and education and the broader cultural framework within which Korean society operated. Whilst much of this can be deduced from the source it also must be recognised the source has limitations. Since the account is autobiographical, the authors own interests and anxieties may have influenced the source. It must also be noted that the source may not reflect the normal trend within Korean society, the girls' experiences may have been abnormal for the time.

One aspect of Korean society which can be deduced from the source is a general theme of occupation and repression. The source implies that there is a national difference between the civilians and the ruling bodies. This creates a convincing picture that the country is controlled by a Japanese organisation rather than by the Korean's themselves. This Japanese body which seems to control Korea during this period also appears to be unwanted and foreign to at least a small number of Korean civilians. Reinforcing this idea of occupation is the evidence of repression within Korean society.

Another aspect of Korean society which can be deduced from the source is how childhood was viewed and the role education played in society. The girl certainly appears to be educated. This is strongly demonstrated through the fact she is literate, as the existence of the source proves, and also attends a 'School'. This demonstrates that children were expected to be educated in Korean society since the girls schooling is never questioned as abnormal within the source.

There also appears to be a lack of parental involvement within the schoolgirls' life. The fact this is also never questioned implies it was not completely abnormal for Korea in this time. The girl never mentions her parents and instead consults a "Pastor" for advice. The fact the girl never mentions her parents appears to have a more important leader in her life such as "pastors" and "teachers" implies Korean parents were either physically or emotionally detached from their children.

Another aspect of Korean society which can be deduced from the source is the role which history and tradition played within Korean society. History seems to be highly valued within Korean society. The fact history appears to be so fundamental to Korean identity perhaps explains why "the Japanese" appear to be trying to repress it.

There also appears to be a harsh justice system, in which capital and corporal punishment are used. The fact this form of harsh justice may be used on young school children also implies that children were seen to be mature and capable of guilt, at least in terms of crime and punishment.

Finally, the source also reveals a more general cultural framework within which Korean society functioned. There appears to be a religious aspect of society. The fact Pastors exist is strong evidence to suggest religion exists. However, the girl herself never actually mentions how much influence religious practice held within Korean society. For example, there is no mention of a religious service or practise and so society may not have been in general very religious.

In conclusion, much about Korean society can be deduced and learnt from the source, the occupation and repression from a Japanese ruling body, childhood and education, the role and importance of written history within society and finally the broader cultural framework of Korea during this period. Whilst the source does have limitations, mainly the unverified accuracy of the author's descriptions, the personal interests of the author and also the narrow outlook it offers, the source is still useful in determining many aspects of the Korean society and culture

We'll break it down and take a look at this one paragraph at a time.

The source describes a girl's experiences at a school in Korea during the early half of the twentieth century. The source is written in the first-person past tense, thus implying that the events described in the source are the personal memories of the author. This autobiographical account can reveal a lot of Korean society and culture during this period. For example, the source describes themes of occupation and repression, the role which history and tradition played in society, childhood and education and the broader cultural framework within which Korean society operated. Whilst much of this can be deduced from the source it also must be recognised the source has limitations. Since the account is autobiographical, the authors own interests and anxieties may have influenced the source. It must also be noted that the source may not reflect the normal trend within Korean society, the girls' experiences may have been abnormal for the time.

The above paragraph serves as the introduction. There's no real issue with providing evidence here because in the introduction you can just summarise your main points without the need to provide evidence. However, in the subsequent paragraphs when each of these points are laid out individually, they do need to be evidenced.

One aspect of Korean society which can be deduced from the source is a general theme of occupation and repression. The source implies that there is a national difference between the civilians and the ruling bodies. This creates a convincing picture that the country is controlled by a Japanese organisation rather than by the Korean's themselves. This Japanese body which seems to control Korea during this period also appears to be unwanted and foreign to at least a small number of Korean civilians. Reinforcing this idea of occupation is the evidence of repression within Korean society.

In this paragraph, the candidate is making a point about Korea being occupied and controlled by the Japanese, an occupation which is unwelcome. While we may be able to draw the same conclusions from the text, there needs to be evidence in here. For example, they could mention the existence of the "Japanese police" who may have been told of the girls' "crimes", which you can explain the relevance of. You can do the same thing by referring to the fact that the Pastor warns the girl that "the Japanese" will punish her. There could also be a reference to the 'secret hiding place' and 'smuggling' a history book to more clearly demonstrate the repression apparent in society, and you can link it to a Japanese source by pointing to the fact that this smuggling was targeted at Korean 'patriotic young men'.

Another aspect of Korean society which can be deduced from the source is how childhood was viewed and the role education played in society. The girl certainly appears to be educated. This is strongly demonstrated through the fact she is literate, as the existence of the source proves, and also attends a 'School'. This demonstrates that children were expected to be educated in Korean society since the girls schooling is never questioned as abnormal within the source.

Again, the point being made here might be potentially valid, though there is a real risk of the author inferring points from absence. Here, the only piece of evidence which has been provided by the candidate is their mentioning of a 'school'. You could also talk about evidence for education coming from the existence of the source, and the relationship between the schoolgirls, their teacher, and their work copying out complex texts.

There also appears to be a lack of parental involvement within the schoolgirls' life. The fact this is also never questioned implies it was not completely abnormal for Korea in this time. The girl never mentions her parents and instead consults a "Pastor" for advice. The fact the girl never mentions her parents appears to have a more important leader in her life such as "pastors" and "teachers" implies Korean parents were either physically or emotionally detached from their children.

This paragraph is an interesting example of inference from absence. The candidate has made a real mistake here by using the lack of evidence for something to prove that the opposite is true. If you can only support your point by citing the fact that the source doesn't mention the opposite of your point, it's not worth making. It looks like the candidate made the point without being able to identify any evidence to back it up!

Another aspect of Korean society which can be deduced from the source is the role which history and tradition played within Korean society. History seems to be highly valued within Korean society. The fact history appears to be so fundamental to Korean identity perhaps explains why "the Japanese" appear to be trying to repress it.

This is a good point, it might even be one of the most important points to take from the source; that Korean society valued history highly, and that the Japanese were keen to suppress Korean history as part of their occupation. There is a real lack of evidence though, the candidate just mentions that the Japanese are trying to repress it, rather than how this is shown. The candidate could include things like the value the pastor places on the book, the fact that it had to be hidden, and that it was distributed to study groups which would eventually form resistance cells to back up their point.

There also appears to be a harsh justice system, in which capital and corporal punishment are used. The fact this form of harsh justice may be used on young school children also implies that children were seen to be mature and capable of guilt, at least in terms of crime and punishment.

This is a small, but valid point, which again could be elevated considerably by bringing in direct reference to the source, for example, talking about how the girl may be "jailed, possibly beaten, perhaps even killed" and explaining that punishing children in such a way demonstrates a society marked by a severe justice system.

Finally, the source also reveals a more general cultural framework within which Korean society functioned. There appears to be a religious aspect of society. The fact Pastors exist is strong evidence to suggest religion exists. However, the girl herself never actually mentions how much influence religious practice held within Korean society. For example, there is no mention of a religious service or practise and so society may not have been in general very religious.

Our last point is a good observation about religion in Korean society and culture. This could hit some high-level indicators, but the lack of evidence blocks that. The candidate could bring in the existence of the pastor, as well as "spiritual leaders" who were guiding "secret study circles". Again, we have another case here of inference from absence, as the candidate has used the lack of any descriptions of religious services to argue that they were not common, which just doesn't work. Focusing on the role of the pastor and other religious leaders could convincingly support a point that religious figures were important in Korean society and culture, particularly with regards to anti-Japanese resistance.

In conclusion, much about Korean society can be deduced and learnt from the source, the occupation and repression from a Japanese ruling body, childhood and education, the role and importance of written history within society and finally the broader cultural framework of Korea during this period. Whilst the source does have limitations, mainly the unverified accuracy of the author's descriptions, the personal interests of the author and also the narrow outlook it offers, the source is still useful in determining many aspects of the Korean society and culture

The conclusion doesn't need to bring in specific evidence, like the introduction, and this conclusion is quite good as a result! There is a reinforcing of existing points and an answer to the question.

This response, in its current form, would not be able to get much about 20/40 marks. However, by adding in more evidence, that can go up. Let's look at an improved version:

The source describes a girl's experiences at a school in Korea during the early half of the twentieth century. For example, the source describes themes of occupation and repression, the role which history and tradition played in society, childhood and education and the broader cultural framework within which Korean society operated. Whilst much of this can be deduced from the source it also must be recognised the source has limitations. The source may not reflect the normal trend within Korean society, the girls' experiences may have been abnormal for the time.

One aspect of Korean society which can be deduced from the source is a general theme of occupation and repression. The source implies that there is a national difference between the civilians and the ruling bodies. For example, it is mentioned that "Japanese Police" may have to be told of the girls' 'crimes'. This implies that Korean police are either non-existent or lack jurisdictional power to intervene. This is further reinforced when the pastor warns the girl "the Japanese" would punish her. This creates a convincing picture that the country is controlled by a Japanese organisation rather than by the Koreans themselves. This Japanese body which seems to control Korea during this period also appears to be unwanted and foreign to at least a small number of Korean civilians. The girl mentions a "resistance" against the Japanese, thus implying the Japanese presence is unwanted, otherwise, why would a resistance movement exist. This further reinforces the theme of foreign occupation or rule.

Reinforcing this idea of occupation is the evidence of repression within Korean society. The existence of a "secret hiding place" combined with the fact the girl "smuggled" her Korean history book out of the school, suggests that these items where prohibited. This prohibition also appears to have been implemented by the Japanese, since the Pastor and "patriotic young men" use the girls smuggled goods for the resistance.

Another aspect of Korean society which can be deduced from the source is how childhood was viewed and the role education played in society. The girl certainly appears to be educated. This is strongly demonstrated through the fact she is literate, as the existence of the source proves, and also attends a school. The girl also appears to be or have become multi-lingual since she "translated" various Korean words into English. This demonstrates that children were expected to be educated in Korean society since the girls schooling is never questioned as abnormal within the source. Furthermore, the girls' rapport with Miss Golden and the way that she sought to protect them implies that teachers played a significant role in the life of many young people in Korea.

Another aspect of Korean society which can be deduced from the source is the role which history and tradition played within Korean society. History seems to be highly valued within Korean society. The girl is told to value a Korean history book, with the pastor telling her to "love it, cherish it, protect it". This idea that history is important within Korean society is further reinforced when the girl is told her efforts to preserve Korean history are comparable to "saving Korea". The fact history appears to be so fundamental to Korean identity perhaps explains why "the Japanese" appear to be trying to repress it.

There also appears to be a harsh justice system, in which capital and corporal punishment are used. This is demonstrated in the text when it is mentioned the schoolgirls may be "jailed, possibly beaten, perhaps even killed". The fact this form of harsh justice may be used on young school children also implies that crimes were punished severely, and in this case the possession and distribution of Korean history was such a severe crime that children could be corporally or capitally punished.

Finally, the source also reveals a more general cultural framework within which Korean society functioned. There appears to be a religious aspect of society. The girl identifies "Pastor Kim" and also reveals that "spiritual leaders" help lead "secret study circles". The fact Pastors exist alongside other spiritual leaders, who are seemingly centres of Korean identity and a young male militant group, suggests that Koreans valued the role played by religious figures and possibly religion itself.

In conclusion, much about Korean society can be deduced and learnt from the source, the occupation and repression from a Japanese ruling body, childhood and education, the role and importance of written history within society and finally the broader cultural framework of Korea during this period.

This answer is much higher, placing in mid-30s, and would meet the threshold for consideration for interview!

AVOIDING REDUNDANCY

In HAT responses, redundancy is quite simply when you make the same point more than once. It is important to avoid this because it takes up valuable writing time, and it looks to the examiner like you don't really know what point you are making.

The easiest way to avoid this is simple. Make sure your plan doesn't cover the same point more than once and then make sure that you stick to your plan. It's as simple as that! Sometimes you can use the same piece of evidence to make different points, but to avoid redundancy by making sure that all of your points are different!

QUOTATION DO'S AND DON'TS

Many candidates like to use quotations to point to the evidence they are using in the original passage. While this is not absolutely necessary, it is a very easy way to demonstrate what you are referring to. However, candidates often misuse quotations and there are a few simple tips we have included here to help you minimise this when you are writing out your answers.

The first one is not to overquote. Overquoting is where you either quote large pieces of text or quote lots of small bits in short order. For example, you want to avoid paragraphs like:

> **The author's cultural values are clearly shown by "the scintillating nature of Icatian culture outshines all other cultures around the world, from our scouts to our magistrates we are truly preeminent in art, learning, and numbers."**

or, indeed:

> **The author's cultural values are clearly shown by his allusions to the "scintillating" nature of "Icatian culture" and how it "outshines" many other cultures in the "world".**

as these are both examples of overquoting. They don't look good and don't read well. It is better to use a small number of short, precise quotations to back up your claims, and generally only if they say things in the source which you feel you could not say better. You can also, for example, paraphrase what the author describes, and only use a quotation to bring up a specific phrase or even word that they are using which you think is particularly relevant ("outshines" may be a good one, but "world" is not).

If you can quote appropriately, you can still trip up on your grammar and punctuation. Always make sure that you introduce a quote by clarifying that this is something the author thinks. For example, you could say something like:

> **The author's cultural values are clearly shown by the fact that he considers Icatian culture to "outshine" other cultures, and therefore believes it to be superior in a number of fields, including the arts and mathematics.**

When punctuating your quotations, you should use either single inverted commas (' ') or double quotation marks (" ") in order to denote the start and end of your quotation. The important thing to remember is to **remain consistent** throughout your essay.

If your quotations contain punctuation, this should be duplicated in your quotation. If you want to say that the author describes Icatian excellence in "art, learning, and numbers" you must leave those commas in.

Sometimes, if your quotation comes at the end of a sentence. It this happens, you should put a full stop after you end your quotation, so

> **The author clearly feels that the Icatians are culturally superior throughout their society, spanning "our scouts to our magistrates".**

If you are ending your sentence with a quotation which, itself, is the end of the sentence, the full stop moves from outside the quotation marks to inside.

Sometimes, you might feel that you need to include a larger part of a quotation, but want to avoid overquoting. You can do this by breaking up the punctuation using an ellipsis (...) these show the reader that something is missing from the quotation, and allows you to include larger passages without overquoting:

> **The author makes it clear that he believes Icatian culture to have a "scintillating nature... in art, learning, and numbers."**

ANALYSING, NOT DESCRIBING

Teachers and guides alike will often stress the importance of being analytical rather than descriptive. While this is true, it is useless if you don't know what they mean.

To write analytically, you need to provide a particular argument about the material you are discussing, rather than just saying what the author says, use what they are saying to make points of your own, and support them with evidence.

The key requirements for writing analytically are clearly understanding the requirements of the question, ensuring that each point you make contributes towards answering that question, having a clear answer to the question and sticking to it, and supporting your points throughout your writing by referring back to the source. All of these are things we've already shown you how to do, so hopefully you can write analytically really well by this point!

LINKING TO THE QUESTION

Once you have made a point in your paragraph, supported it with evidence, and explained your thinking, you need to create a link back to your original question. This shows the examiner just how the point you've made contributes to your greater argument, and can really help them understand your work.

The easiest way to do this is to *use the language of the question* to shape your link. For instance, if the question in your HAT wants you to write about what the source can tell you about the society and culture of 19th century London, then a question link might end a paragraph with:

> **It is clear, then, that the culture of 19th century London was undergoing significant change as the population grew and diversified, and that much of this change was unpopular with the residents.**

By using the actual wording of the question, we have made it clear that the point and supporting evidence we have used are directly responding to what's being asked of us, we are talking about culture in 19th century London, and we are *showing* that to the examiner.

If you can make links like this, it will really help the examiner understand what you are doing, and it will also force you, while you write, to double-check that each of your points *has* a clear link back to the question, which it must do!

SHOWING YOUR THINKING

We've demonstrated several times before that it is important to make sure that you clearly communicate your reasoning when you are writing. Just like you would in a maths exam, you have to show your working in order to get the highest possible marks.

There is no special trick to this particularly, but it is very important. For each point you make, you need to make sure that you provide evidence to support that point, as we've already covered. However, the link that exists in your mind between the evidence and the point is not always apparent, and so you should make sure that you always take the time to explain why all of your evidence is supporting your point.

You don't always have to address each piece of evidence in turn, often you can just explain your thinking with all of them by saying something like "all of these suggest that they were trading in valuable items, which were consumable and illicit and therefore that the missionaries in Baghdad were engaging with some form of black market."

A useful trick to help you to remember to do this is to assume that the examiner reading your HAT paper doesn't know anything about the passage you've read or the topic. If they didn't have a copy of the test in front of them, they would have no way to understand how your points worked unless you explained it to them, and that's just what you need to do. If you can manage that then the clarity and quality of your written answers will improve, as will your final mark!

GOOD ENGLISH

One of the criteria which will be factored into the marking of your exam, and the ease with which your examiner can give you a good mark, is through good use of the English language. Remember, this is an aptitude test, and they want to make sure that you can flourish in a very writing and reading-heavy subject at Oxford.

The examiners will be looking for you to demonstrate fluent English, including good use of vocabulary, good sentence structure, and sound use of grammar. They will also want you to make sure that you spell words correctly, and appropriately punctuate your sentences.

Under the time limits and pressure of the exam, it is inevitable that you will make a mistake or two. This will not derail your result, but if you make more than a few mistakes this can begin to add up quickly, so try your best to avoid such errors.

Our top tip for developing these skills if you are concerned? Read. Read loads, particularly in print, as novels and printed newspapers tend to have better standards of English than online resources. In the exam, a good way to minimise the number of mistakes you make is to check over your answer once you have written it, and correcting any language errors that you spot, as well as any errors with your conclusion.

*HAT Survival tip: If you are more than half way through your essay, and you realise that you have made a **serious** mistake, don't stop. There isn't time to start your essay again. Instead, focus on trying to show the best points you have identified, evidence them well, explain clearly, and demonstrate how they relate to the question. This will produce a better final result than scrapping your entire answer and starting again if you're over the halfway mark.*

Another important thing to note is about clarity. Tons of HAT students try really hard to 'sound clever' by using unnecessarily complicated words and phrases. The HAT examiners want you to show that you have a good vocabulary by interacting with complex vocabulary in the passage, not by bringing in your own. ***The easier it is to understand you, the higher your mark will be.*** Often, candidates who try to sound clever give the impression of trying to bamboozle the examiners. This is incredibly risky, as the examiners tend to be experienced Oxford academics who have marked hundreds or thousands of exams, essays, and dissertations. They know when someone is trying to show off, or hide behind language, and it doesn't work. Our top tip here: write as accessibly as possible for the best chance at good marks.

TIMING

In this guide we've talked about the importance of unpacking the question, carefully reading the source, *twice*, analysing the source, planning your answer, and then writing it.

All of this has to take place in one hour. The exact timing that works for you will depend on how quickly you can complete each of these sections. Some candidates will write much more quickly than others, while some can read and analyse very quickly. We will try to give you a detailed breakdown of timing for the HAT, however, which you can use as a guide:

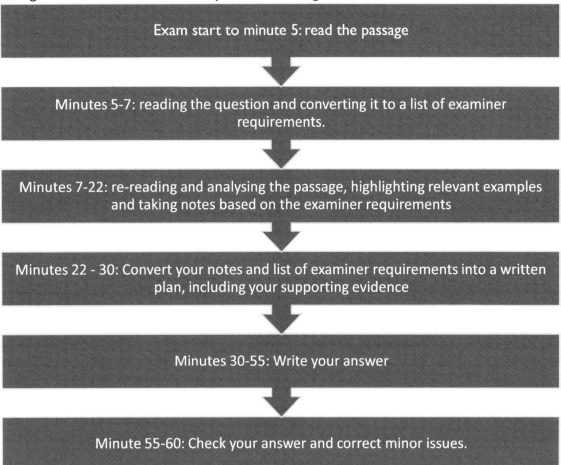

Exam start to minute 5: read the passage

Minutes 5-7: reading the question and converting it to a list of examiner requirements.

Minutes 7-22: re-reading and analysing the passage, highlighting relevant examples and taking notes based on the examiner requirements

Minutes 22 - 30: Convert your notes and list of examiner requirements into a written plan, including your supporting evidence

Minutes 30-55: Write your answer

Minute 55-60: Check your answer and correct minor issues.

In our plan, you start writing exactly halfway through the exam. This may seem quite alarmingly late! It's important to remember though that the examiners are expecting around two sides of A4 paper. If you write, without interruption (because you'll already know exactly what you will say from your plan), most people can easily write that much in 25 minutes. If you cannot, then add extra time.

If you have access arrangements which mean that you get extra time for the exam, then you can expand each section of this plan depending on where you need the most time.

HAT SURVIVAL ESSENTIALS – UNDERSTANDING THE HAT MARK SCHEME

BANDS

HAT responses are broken down into four bands: from Exemplary to Good, to Fair, to Poor. The majority of candidates are in the Exemplary band, but far from exclusively. Many candidates also come from the Good band, and a few even from Fair.

In order to maximise your chances of securing an interview, and an eventual offer and place, you want to be aiming for Exemplary. To hit Exemplary, you need 82.5% or around 33/40 marks. Only a small number of candidates hit this tier each year.

For a Good band answer you will need at least 57%, or 23/40. The average pass mark for candidates invited to interview is around 70%, or partway through the Good band. These averages move each year depending on the difficulty of the question and the aptitude of yourself and your colleagues, which is why we strongly advise that you don't aim for something around 70%, but in fact, aim for the Exemplary band to maximise your odds of making the interview threshold.

Anything below 50% is a Fair answer, in which your odds of being invited to interview are very slim, though not zero. The odds are certainly not in your favour here, so you want to make sure that you can avoid that, and the even worse Poor answer.

To do that, the best piece of advice is to practice and develop the skills detailed in this guide, make use of our practice papers, and the HAT papers available online. It might also help to know just what each band requires so that you can picture just what the HAT examiner will see while they are marking your work, and you can make sure that you are reliably hitting it.

For the Exemplary tier, the examiners are specifically looking for your response to the HAT question to be a direct answer to the question which is extremely well organised and reasoned. They want to see you clearly examining the implications of the passage individually, and then bringing them all together into a single narrative flow. They want to see you intelligently deal with issues of authorship, sphere and meaning. A really useful tip to remember here is that you need to consider all of the evidence which is relevant to the question, even that which seems to contradict other pieces. Those contradictions and tensions within the source are things that you should mention, and even make points out of, if you can.

As a part of that, exemplary answers require you to show that you can read the passage 'intelligently and perceptively'. This is a slightly vague term, meaning that they want you to be able to make logical connections between what is said in the passage and what you can assume, based on that, about the author's world. Think about the work you've done on suspending disbelief, making assumptions from the content, from the author, and from the source's existence, those are all places that you can demonstrate how clever you are by *working out things from the source which aren't explicitly said by the source*. The final requirement for a top tier answer is based on level indicators. If you have a very small number of low-level indicators, and a very high number of high-level indicators, it's very likely that your response will be considered exemplary.

EXAMINER'S TIPS - HOW TO MAXIMISE GREAT INDICATORS, AND MINIMISE POOR ONES.

Level indicators vary from year to year and are based on each specific passage. A lot of them hinge on being able to make those intelligent, perceptive interpretations of the source. There will be specific examples which the examiners have in mind, although while they might like you to hit those, they do not require you to do so in order to get a high-level indicator.

This means that you can **almost guarantee creating high-level indicators for yourself** provided that you are able to make intelligent deductions about the author's world in relation to the question, and which you can clearly back up by showing your thinking and linking to the passage.

That's one group of high-level indicators. The next is more generic and focuses on your ability to *demonstrate* your interaction with the passage. If you understand it really well, that's great, but you need to also show the examiner that you're bringing in evidence from throughout the passage and using it to support your argument. To that end, you should try to make sure that in all of your HAT responses, you:

> Always make sure that you interact with material from the entire length of the source. You don't have to talk about all of the material, there isn't the time or space, but you do have to show you've not just looked at the beginning, middle, or end.

> Show that the evidence you are using is appropriate to the point you are making. Don't just grab random quotes, use the highlighting you made on your second reading and identify what gave you the idea for your current point, see what supports your point the most.

> Deploy your evidence in an impartial and objective manner. A crucial skill of historians is to report on and interpret the past while minimising the damage their own biases do. Make observations without *judging* it in any particular way.

> Don't bring in any external knowledge. Just don't.

> Don't overquote - the examiners have a specific high-level indicator requiring students to paraphrase wherever possible. As we covered in the Quotation do's and don'ts, it should only be used when you couldn't say it better yourself.

Similarly, there are set high-level indicators for your writing style and structure; these might vary slightly year on year, but basically remain the same. Again, this means that if you learn to do them, you will increase your chances of getting a lot of high-level indicators!

> The first thing is to **answer the question.** This has been covered thoroughly in the 'How to read questions' section of HAT Basics (page 26)

> The next is establishing clear definitions, where required, and using those to directly address the relevant active elements of the question.

> You also need to make sure that your answer is broken up into distinct paragraphs, that each paragraph has a clear and distinct theme, and that you have organised those paragraphs into an order which makes sense.

> Write clearly. This means that you should make sure that you are using good English, it also means that you should not be using unnecessarily complex words, sentences, clauses or phrases.

These are all things which will apply to any HAT exam. If you can hit most or all of these specific ones, as well as making sure that you're making intelligent observations in support of your argument and backed up by clear logical links to the evidence, you'll be on track for loads of high-level indicators.

For that Exemplary tier though, that's only half of the battle. You also need a relative minority of low-level indicators. For a lot of candidates, avoiding those is a much harder thing to wrap their head around. Many of them are obvious opposites to the high-level indicators, but some notable ones to avoid include:

> Being descriptive, rather than analytical (covered on page 83)

> Arguing the passage 'can't tell us much' or similar, because of its limitations. (The passage is all you have for the HAT, so the examiner's know just what you can get out of it, it's never going to be a trick).

> Failing to identify and discuss the source's limitations

> Not discussing or responding to inconsistencies within the material, and not showing your understanding that your argument can never be absolute.

Trying to judge whether part or all of the source is 'true'

Misunderstanding the meaning of part of the text

Making too few distinct points about the active elements in the question/ focusing on a single issue.

Failing to understand the requirements of the question (covered on page 29)

Structuring your essay so it follows the passage. Your paragraphs should follow a narrative flow which you have chosen to best answer the question, rather than just being arranged from "first appears in the passage" to "last appears in the passage"

WHAT'S NEXT?

The next section of this book includes a number of original practice HAT papers which we have created for you to practice on. We have also included sample answers, all of which have mistakes included which we have clearly pointed out and shown solutions for to help you understand and avoid a lot of the pitfalls.

Try out each of these questions yourself, refer back to the previous sections of this book if you are ever struggling with analysing the source, or understanding the question. Use them to work out what timings are best for you, how long you need for each section, and practice your reading and source analysis.

You can also try your hand at the actual HAT past papers, there are a number available online from https://www.history.ox.ac.uk/history-aptitude-test-hat. If you can, save these until last, and practice them in timed conditions. If you can, ask your history teacher to look over one or two of the answers you write to those papers, and they may be able to help you refine your answer.

All you need to do really well in the HAT is in this guide, so here should be your first start. Make sure that you understand the ins and outs of questions and source analysis. Make sure that you can reliably plan out answers and organise them effectively, and strive to hit as many high-level indicators as you can. If you can do that, you'll be well on your way to HAT success.

EXAMPLE PAPERS WITH PRACTICE ANSWERS

MOCK A

NOTE: This test is made up of one question, based on a passage from an historical source. You do not need to know anything about the author of the source or the context in which he was writing to answer the question. Candidates will be penalised for making use of any outside knowledge.

The following is an extract from a letter written by the leader of the EZLN rebellion, Subcomandante Marcos, to national and local press in the immediate aftermath of their armed uprising against the Mexican government in January 1994. The Rebellion began in the south-western Mexican state of Chiapas where there is a large indigenous population. The text discusses the current state of the EZLN and the problems they face. Candidates do not need to know anything about the EZLN uprising or Mexican politics or society to answer this question and they should not attempt to draw on outside knowledge.

January 13, 1994

To the national newspaper La Jornada:

To the national newspaper El Financiero:

Dear Gentlemen:

The EZLN has produced a series of documents and communique's that may be of interest to the national and international press. My compañeros in the EZLN have asked me to find a way for these documents [of January 6, 11, 12, and 13] to reach their destinations and be made known to the public. For this we turn to you, to ask if it is possible for you, through your means, to put these documents into the public domain. These documents contain our position on the events that occurred between January 7-13, 1994. I clarify this because, to reach you, the documents packet must travel for days, crossing mountains and valleys and bypassing tanks, military vehicles, thousands of men dressed in olive-green uniforms, and all of the war arsenal with which they try to intimidate us. They forget that war is not a matter of weapons or a large number of armed men, but of politics. Anyway, the fact is that these documents and this letter will take a few days to reach you, that is, if they reach you.

We are fine, and in these documents we reiterate our disposition to dialogue to find a just solution to this conflict. At the same time, we are somewhat immobile as a result of all the military paraphernalia with which the government is trying to cover up the injustice and corruption that our actions have exposed. The peace which some now ask for has been a constant battle for us. It seems that Mexico's powerful men are bothered by the fact that Indians now go to die in the cities and stain their streets, which up till now were only littered with wrappers from imported products. They would rather they continue to die in the mountains, far from good consciences and tourists.

It will not be like this any longer. The well-being of a few cannot be based on the suffering of the masses. Now they will have to share our luck, for better or for worse. They have had previous opportunities to turn around and do something about the nation's historic injustice against its original inhabitants, but they saw them as nothing more than anthropological objects, touristic curiosities, or part of a "Jurassic park" (is that how you spell it?) that fortunately would disappear with a North American Free Trade Agreement[1] that did not include them, except as disposable elements. Because in Mexico, death in the mountains still doesn't count. Everyone is guilty, from the highest-level federal functionaries to the last of the corrupt "Indigenous" leaders, and including a governor who was not elected by Chiapanecos[2] according to their will and right, municipal presidents more concerned with ornamental works and strengthening relations with powerful men than with governing for their people, and officials on all levels, who deny the people who inhabited these lands even before they did, health, education, land, housing, services, just employment, food, justice, and most importantly, respect and dignity. They have forgotten that human dignity is not only the right of those who have their basic living conditions resolved, but also those who have no material belongings to differentiate themselves from things and animals: dignity. But it is just to recognize that in the middle of this sea of indifference there have been and are voices that have spoken about the misery that these injustices bring. Among these voices was and is that of honest journalism, which still exists locally and nationally. Actually, why do I bore you? It seems that you already have enough problems trying to convince the Federal Army to let you do your jobs. In sum, what we want is peace with dignity and justice.

Their tanks, planes, helicopters, and thousands of soldiers don't frighten us. The same injustices that they force upon us--no roads or basic services--are now being turned against them. We don't need roads, because we have always gotten around on footpaths. Not even with all their federal soldiers would they be able to close off all the paths that our misery once used, and that now are used by our rebellion. We also are not affected by the lies presented by television and in the press. Do they forget the illiteracy rate in the state of Chiapas? How many houses have no electricity and thus no televisions in these lands? If the nation falls for these lies again, there will always be at least one of us who is prepared to awaken them again. The Clandestine Revolutionary Indigenous Committees[3] are indestructible. Since their formation they have had a command register. If one or several fall, another or several others will take their places and their future relief will sign up. They will have to annihilate all of us, absolutely every last one of us, in order to deter us militarily. And they will always be left with the doubt that they missed one of us, and that person will begin the rebellion all over again.

Will all this serve to teach "the Mexicans" to say "Chiapas" instead of "Chapas" and "Tzeltales[4]" instead of "Setsales"?

Health and an embrace, if there is still a place and a way

Insurgent Subcommander Marcos

What does this extract reveal about politics and society in Chiapas, Mexico in the 1990s?

---

[1] The North American Free Trade Agreement, commonly referred to as NAFTA, was a free trade agreement signed between Mexico and The United States in January 1994.
[2] Chiapanecos simply refers to the people who live in the Mexican state of Chiapas
[3] This refers to the several revolutionary groups that were active in Mexico at the time.
[4] The Tzeltales people are indigenous Mayans who predominantly live in Chiapas.

MOCK B

NOTE: This test is made up of one question, based on a passage from an historical source. You do not need to know anything about the author of the source or the context in which he was writing to answer the question. Candidates will be penalised for making use of any outside knowledge.

This source is a chapter from Mohandas K Gandhi's Hind Swaraj (Indian Home Rule) written in 1909. Gandhi was a prominent figure amongst the wider Indian nationalist movement, gaining particular repute from the late 1910s until his assassination in 1948. Hind Swaraj was a brief pamphlet, originally written in Gandhi's native Gujarati language, taking the form of a dialogue between a 'reader' and an 'editor'. The text is an early meditation on potential forms of 'Hind Swaraj', Indian self-rule, following the possible future advent of independence from British colonial rule. Candidates do not need to know anything about Indian nationalism or British Imperial history and should not attempt to draw on outside knowledge.

Reader: I have now learnt what the Congress[5] has done to make India one nation, how the Partition[6] has caused an awakening, and how discontent and unrest have spread through the land. I would now like to know your views on Swaraj. I fear that our interpretation is not the same as yours.

Editor: It is quite possible that we do not attach the same meaning to the term. You and I and all Indians are impatient to obtain Swaraj, but we are certainly not decided as to what it is. To drive the English out of India is a thought heard from many mouths, but it does not seem that many have properly considered why it should be so. I must ask you a question. Do not think that it is necessary to drive away the English, if we get all we want?

Reader: I should ask of them only one thing, that is: "Please leave our country." If, after they have complied with this request, their withdrawal from India means that they are still in India, I should have no objection. Then we would understand that, in their language, the word "gone" is equivalent to "remained".

Editor: Well then, let us suppose that the English have retired. What will you do then?

Reader: That question cannot be answered at this stage. The state after withdrawal will depend largely upon the manner of it. If, as you assume, they retire, it seems to me we shall still keep their constitution and shall carry on the Government. If they simply retire for the asking we should have an army, etc., ready at hand. We should, therefore, have no difficulty in carrying on the Government.

Editor: You may think so; I do not. But I will not discuss the matter just now. I have to answer your question, and that I can do well by asking you several questions. Why do you want to drive away the English?

Reader: Because India has become impoverished by their Government. They take away our money from year to year. The most important posts are reserved for themselves. We are kept in a state of slavery. They behave insolently towards us and disregard our feelings.

---

[5] Congress refers to the Indian National Congress founded in 1885. Congress was the primary vehicle for anticolonial nationalism in the late 19th and 20th Century.
[6] Partition refers to the split of Bengal Province in 1905 at the hands of the Raj.

Editor: If they do not take our money away, become gentle, and give us responsible posts, would you still consider their presence to be harmful?

Reader: That question is useless. It is similar to the question whether there is any harm in associating with a tiger if he changes his nature. Such a question is sheer waste of time. When a tiger changes his nature, Englishmen will change theirs. This is not possible, and to believe it to be possible is contrary to human experience.

Editor: Supposing we get Self-Government similar to what the Canadians and the South Africans have, will it be good enough?

Reader: That question also is useless. We may get it when we have the same powers; we shall then hoist our own flag. As is Japan, so must India be. We must own our navy, our army, and we must have our own splendour, and then will India's voice ring through the world.

Editor: You have drawn the picture well. In effect it means this; that we want English rule without the Englishman. You want the tiger's nature, but not the tiger; that is to say, you would make India English. And when it becomes English, it will be called not Hindustan but Englistan. This is not the Swaraj that I want.

Reader: I have placed before you my idea of Swaraj as I think it should be. If the education we have received be of any use, if the works of Spencer, Mill[7] and others be of any importance, and if the English Parliament be the Mother of Parliaments, I certainly think that we should copy the English people, and this to such an extent that, just as they do not allow others to obtain a footing in their country, so we should not allow them or others to obtain it in ours. What they have done in their own country has not been done in any other country. It is, therefore, proper for us to import their institutions. But now I want to know your views.

Editor: There is a need for patience. My views will develop of themselves in the course of this discourse. It is as difficult for me to understand the true nature of Swaraj as it seems to you to be easy. I shall, therefore, for the time being, content myself with endeavouring to show that what you call Swaraj is not truly Swaraj.

What does this extract reveal about the nature of early anti-colonial nationalism in India?

---

[7] John Stuart Mill and Herbert Spencer were highly influential British political philosophers/orientalist scholars who had written about India at length. Their ideas, notably Mill's utilitarianism, were formative in shaping the contours of British colonial rule.

MOCK C

NOTE: This test is made up of one question, based on a passage from an historical source. You do not need to know anything about the author of the source or the context in which he was writing to answer the question. Candidates will be penalised for making use of any outside knowledge.

The following is an extract from Thomas More's 'Utopia'. Thomas More was a prominent lawyer in Tudor England and rose to prominence during the reign of Henry VIII. His book Utopia is a work of socio-political fiction which depicts a fictional island society and their political, social, and religious practices. Candidates do not need to know anything about Thomas More or Tudor religious ideas and should not attempt to draw on outside knowledge.

"There are several sorts of religions, not only in different parts of the island, but even in every town; some worshipping the sun, others the moon or one of the planets. Some worship such men as have been eminent in former times for virtue or glory, not only as ordinary deities, but as the supreme god. Yet the greater and wiser sort of them worship none of these, but adore one eternal, invisible, infinite, and incomprehensible Deity; as a Being that is far above all our apprehensions, that is spread over the whole universe, not by His bulk, but by His power and virtue; Him they call the Father of All, and acknowledge that the beginnings, the increase, the progress, the vicissitudes, and the end of all things come only from Him; nor do they offer divine honours to any but to Him alone. And, indeed, though they differ concerning other things, yet all agree in this: that they think there is one Supreme Being that made and governs the world, whom they call, in the language of their country, Mithras[1]. They differ in this: that one thinks the god whom he worships is this Supreme Being, and another thinks that his idol is that god; but they all agree in one principle, that whoever is this Supreme Being, He is also that great essence to whose glory and majesty all honours are ascribed by the consent of all nations."

"By degrees they fall off from the various superstitions that are among them, and grow up to that one religion that is the best and most in request; and there is no doubt to be made, but that all the others had vanished long ago, if some of those who advised them to lay aside their superstitions had not met with some unhappy accidents, which, being considered as inflicted by heaven, made them afraid that the god whose worship had like to have been abandoned had interposed and revenged themselves on those who despised their authority."

---

[1] **Mithras** the Iranian **god** of the sun, justice, contract, and war in ancient Iran. He was also known as Mithras in the Roman Empire during the 2nd and 3rd centuries AD, this deity was honoured as the patron of loyalty to the emperor

"After they had heard from us an account of the doctrine, the course of life, and the miracles of Christ, and of the wonderful constancy of so many martyrs, whose blood, so willingly offered up by them, was the chief occasion of spreading their religion over a vast number of nations, it is not to be imagined how inclined they were to receive it. I shall not determine whether this proceeded from any secret inspiration of God, or whether it was because it seemed so favourable to that community of goods, which is an opinion so particular as well as so dear to them; since they perceived that Christ and His followers lived by that rule, and that it was still kept up in some communities among the sincerest sort of Christians. From whichsoever of these motives it might be, true it is, that many of them came over to our religion, and were initiated into it by baptism. But as two of our number were dead, so none of the four that survived were in priests' orders, we, therefore, could only baptise them, so that, to our great regret, they could not partake of the other sacraments, that can only be administered by priests, but they are instructed concerning them and long most vehemently for them. They have had great disputes among themselves, whether one chosen by them to be a priest would not be thereby qualified to do all the things that belong to that character, even though he had no authority derived from the Pope, and they seemed to be resolved to choose some for that employment, but they had not done it when I left them."

"Those among them that have not received our religion do not fright any from it, and use none ill that goes over to it, so that all the while I was there one man was only punished on this occasion. He being newly baptised did, notwithstanding all that we could say to the contrary, dispute publicly concerning the Christian religion, with more zeal than discretion, and with so much heat, that he not only preferred our worship to theirs, but condemned all their rites as profane, and cried out against all that adhered to them as impious and sacrilegious persons, that were to be damned to everlasting burnings. Upon his having frequently preached in this manner he was seized, and after trial he was condemned to banishment, not for having disparaged their religion, but for his inflaming the people to sedition; for this is one of their most ancient laws, that no man ought to be punished for his religion. At the first constitution of their government, Utopus having understood that before his coming among them the old inhabitants had been engaged in great quarrels concerning religion, by which they were so divided among themselves, that he found it an easy thing to conquer them, since, instead of uniting their forces against him, every different party in religion fought by themselves. After he had subdued them he made a law that every man might be of what religion he pleased, and might endeavour to draw others to it by the force of argument and by amicable and modest ways, but without bitterness against those of other opinions; but that he ought to use no other force but that of persuasion, and was neither to mix with it reproaches nor violence; and such as did otherwise were to be condemned to banishment or slavery."

There is also a solemn and severe law against those who as should so far degenerate from the dignity of human nature, as to think that our souls died with our bodies, or that the world was governed by chance, without a wise overruling Providence: for they all formerly believed that there was a state of rewards and punishments to the good and bad after this life; and they now look on those that think otherwise as scarce fit to be counted men, since they degrade so noble a being as the soul, and reckon it no better than a beast's: thus they are far from looking on such men as fit for human society, or to be citizens of a well-ordered commonwealth; since a man of such principles must needs, as oft as he dares do it, despise all their laws and customs: for there is no doubt to be made, that a man who is afraid of nothing but the law, and apprehends nothing after death, will not scruple to break through all the laws of his country, either by fraud or force, when by this means he may satisfy his appetites. They never raise any that hold these maxims, either to honours or offices, nor employ them in any public trust, but despise them, as men of base and sordid minds. Yet they do not punish them, because they lay this down as a maxim, that a man cannot make himself believe anything he pleases; nor do they drive any to dissemble their thoughts by threatenings, so that men are not tempted to lie or disguise their opinions; which being a sort of fraud, is abhorred by the Utopians[2]: they take care indeed to prevent their disputing in defence of these opinions, especially before the common people: but they suffer, and even encourage them to dispute concerning them in private with their priest, and other grave men, being confident that they will be cured of those mad opinions by having reason laid before them."

What does this extract tell us about the author's opinions on religion and religious practices?

---

[2] 'Utopians' are the people who inhabit Utopia.

MOCK D

NOTE: This test is made up of one question, based on a passage from an historical source. You do not need to know anything about the author of the source or the context in which he was writing to answer the question. Candidates will be penalised for making use of any outside knowledge.

The following is an extract from Bocaccio's 'The Decameron'. Bocaccio was an Italian writer in the fourteenth century and is renowned as one of the founders of Italian prose fiction. This book, The Decameron, is a book of allegories and tells the tale of ten Florentines who flee in the wake of a deadly plague and seek solace in a villa on the outskirts of the city. Candidates do not need to know anything about the black plague or Florence in the fourteenth century and should not attempt to draw on outside knowledge.

I say, then, that the years [of the era] of the fruitful Incarnation of the Son of God[1] had attained to the number of one thousand three hundred and forty-eight, when into the notable city of Florence, fair over every other of Italy, there came the death-dealing pestilence[2], which, through the operation of the heavenly bodies or of our own iniquitous dealings, being sent down upon mankind for our correction by the just wrath of God, had some years before appeared in the parts of the East and after having bereft these latter of an innumerable number of inhabitants, extending without cease from one place to another, had now unhappily spread towards the West. And there against no wisdom availing nor human foresight (whereby the city was purged of many impurities by officers deputed to that end and it was forbidden unto any sick person to enter therein and many were the counsels given for the preservation of health) nor yet humble supplications, not once but many times both in ordered processions and on other wise made unto God by devout persons,—about the coming in of the Spring of the aforesaid year, it began on horrible and miraculous wise to show forth its dolorous effects. Yet not as it had done in the East, where, if any bled at the nose, it was a manifest sign of inevitable death; nay, but in men and women alike there appeared, at the beginning of the malady, certain swellings, either on the groin or under the armpits, whereof some waxed of the bigness of a common apple, others like unto an egg, some more and some less, and these the vulgar named plague-boils. From these two parts the aforesaid death-bearing plague-boils proceeded, in brief space, to appear and come indifferently in every part of the body; wherefrom, after a while, the fashion of the contagion began to change into black or livid blotches, which showed themselves in many [first] on the arms and about the thighs and [after spread to] every other part of the person, in some large and sparse and in others small and thick-sown; and like as the plague-boils had been first (and yet were) a very certain token of coming death, even so were these for everyone to whom they came.

---

[1] The Incarnation of the Son of God is Jesus Christ in the Christian Religion.

[2] The city of Florence was struck by the Black Death in 1348.

To the cure of these maladies nor counsel of physician nor virtue of any medicine appeared to avail or profit aught; on the contrary,—whether it was that the nature of the infection suffered it not or that the ignorance of the physicians (of whom, over and above the men of art, the number, both men and women, who had never had any teaching of medicine, was become exceeding great,) availed not to know whence it arose and consequently took not due measures there against,—not only did few recover thereof, but well nigh all died within the third day from the appearance of the aforesaid signs, this sooner and that later, and for the most part without fever or other accident. And this pestilence was the more virulent for that, by communication with those who were sick thereof, it got hold upon the sound, no otherwise than fire upon things dry or greasy, when as they are brought very near thereunto. Nay, the mischief was yet greater; for that not only did converse and consortion with the sick give to the sound infection of cause of common death, but the mere touching of the clothes or of whatsoever other thing had been touched or used of the sick appeared of itself to communicate the malady to the toucher. A marvellous thing to hear is that which I have to tell and one which, had it not been seen of many men's eyes and of mine own, I had scarce dared credit, much less set down in writing, though I had heard it from one worthy of belief. I say, then, that of such efficiency was the nature of the pestilence in question in communicating itself from one to another, that, not only did it pass from man to man, but this, which is much more, it many times visibly did;—to wit, a thing which had pertained to a man sick or dead of the aforesaid sickness, being touched by an animal foreign to the human species, not only infected this latter with the plague, but in a very brief space of time killed it. Of this mine own eyes (as hath a little before been said) had one day, among others, experience on this wise; to wit, that the rags of a poor man, who had died of the plague, being cast out into the public way, two hogs came up to them and having first, after their wont, rooted amain among them with their snouts, took them in their mouths and tossed them about their jaws; then, in a little while, after turning round and round, they both, as if they had taken poison, fell down dead upon the rags with which they had in an ill hour intermeddled.

From these things and many others like unto them or yet stranger divers fears and conceits were begotten in those who abode alive, which well nigh all tended to a very barbarous conclusion, namely, to shun and flee from the sick and all that pertained to them, and thus doing, each thought to secure immunity for himself. Some there were who conceived that to live moderately and keep oneself from all excess was the best defence against such a danger; wherefore, making up their company, they lived removed from every other and shut themselves up in those houses where none had been sick and where living was best; and there, using very temperately of the most delicate viands and the finest wines and eschewing all incontinence, they abode with music and such other diversions as they might have, never suffering themselves to speak with any nor choosing to hear any news from without of death or sick folk. Others, inclining to the contrary opinion, maintained that to carouse and make merry and go about singing and frolicking and satisfy the appetite in everything possible and laugh and scoff at whatsoever befell was a very certain remedy for such an ill. That which they said they put in practice as best they might, going about day and night, now to this tavern, now to that, drinking without stint or measure; and on this wise they did yet more freely in other folk's houses, so but they scented there aught that liked or tempted them, as they might lightly do, for that every one—as he were to live no longer—had abandoned all care of his possessions, as of himself, wherefore the most part of the houses were become common good and strangers used them, when as they happened upon them, like as the very owner might have done; and with all this bestial preoccupation, they still shunned the sick to the best of their power.

What does this extract reveal about society in 14ᵗʰ century Florence?

MOCK E

NOTE: This test is made up of one question, based on a passage from an historical source. You do not need to know anything about the context of the source to answer the question. Candidates will be penalised for making use of any outside knowledge.

The following is an extract taken from an English court case that took place in 1395. It summarises the questioning of John Rykener, a prostitute who dressed as both a man and a women and who worked in the south of England. Candidates do not need to know anything about gender or sexual practices in late fourteenth century England and should not attempt to draw on outside knowledge.

On 11 December, 18 Richard 11. were brought in the presence of John Fressh, Mayor. and the Aldermen[1] of the City of London John Britby of the county of York and John Rykener, calling [himself] Eleanor, having been detected in women's clothing, who were found last Sunday night between the hours of 8 and 9 by certain officials of the, city lying by a certain stall in Soper's Lane committing that detestable unmentionable and ignominious vice[2].

In a separate examination held before the Mayor and Aldermen about the occurrence, John Britby confessed that he was passing through the high road of Cheap on Sunday between the abovementioned hours and accosted John Rykener, dressed up as a woman, thinking he was a woman, asking him as he would a woman if he could commit a libidinous act with her. Requesting money for [his] labor, Rykener consented, and they went together to the aforesaid stall to complete the act, and were captured there during these detestable wrongdoings by the officials and taken to prison.

Following this, John Rykener, was brought here in woman's clothing and questioned about this matter, acknowledging [himself] to have done everything just as John Britby had confessed. Rykener was also asked who had taught him to exercise this vice, and for how long and in what places and with what persons, masculine or feminine, [he] had committed that libidinous and unspeakable act. [He] swore willingly on [his] soul that a certain Anna, the whore of a former servant of Sir Thomas Blount, first taught him to practice this detestable vice in the manner of a woman. [He] further said that a certain Elizabeth Bronderer first dressed him in women's clothing; she also brought her daughter Alice to diverse men for the sake of lust, placing her with those men in their beds at night without light, making her leave early in the morning and showing them the said John Rykener dressed up in women's clothing, calling him Eleanor and saying that they had misbehaved with her.

[He] further said that certain Phillip, rector of Theydon Garnon, had sex with him as with a woman in Elizabeth Bronderer's house outside Bishopsgate, at which time Rykener took away two gowns of Phillip's, and when Phillip requested them from Rykener he said that [he] was the wife of a certain man and that if Phillip wished to ask for them back [he] would make [his] husband bring suit against him.

Rykener further confessed that for five weeks before the feast of St. Michael's last [he] was staying at Oxford, and there, in women's clothing and calling himself Eleanor, worked as an embroideress; and there in the marsh three unsuspecting scholars - of whom one was named Sir William Foxlee, another Sir John, and the third Sir Walter - practiced the abominable vice with him often.

---

[1] An Alderman is an elected official of a local council, often a second in command to the mayor.
[2] The vice in question here is sodomy.

John Rykener further confessed that on Friday before the feast of St. Michael[3] [he] came to Burford in Oxfordshire and there dwelt with a certain John Clerk at the Swan in the capacity of tapster[4] for the next six weeks, during which time two Franciscans[5], one named Brother Michael and the other Brother John, who gave [him] a gold ring, and one Carmelite[6] friar and six foreign men committed the above-said vice with him, of whom one gave Rykener twelve pence, one twenty pence, and one two shillings.

Rykener further confessed that [he] went to Beaconsfield and there, as a man, had sex with a certain Joan, daughter of John Matthew, and also there two foreign Franciscans all had sex with him as a woman.

John Rykener also confessed that after [his] last return to London a certain Sir John, once chaplain at the Church of St. Margaret Pattens, and two other chaplains committed with him the aforementioned vice in the lanes behind St. Katherine's Church by the Tower of London. Rykener further said that he often had sex as a man with many nuns and also had sex as a man with many women both married and otherwise, how many [he] did not know.

Rykener further confessed that many priests had committed that vice with him as with a woman, how many [he] did not know, and said that [he] accommodated priests more readily than other people because they wished to give [him] more than others.

What does this extract tell us about gender and sexual practices in late fourteenth century England?

---

[3] The feast of St Michael is a Christian celebration held at the end of September.
[4] A tapster is a medieval term for a barman or woman.
[5] 'Franciscans' mentioned here is a reference to an order of catholic monks
[6] 'Carmelite' is a reference to particular Christian denomination.

MOCK F

This last paper is provided without a practice answer, so that you can practice it entirely blind, as a final step before moving on to the official past papers.

NOTE: This test is made up of one question, based on a passage from a primary source. You do not need to know anything about the author of the source or the context in which he was writing to answer the question. Candidates will be penalised for making use of any outside knowledge.

This extract is taken from a speech given by Marechal Pétain on the 13th of August 1941 from Vichy, the capital of the unoccupied French territory. The speech marks approximately a year since the German invasion of France and the subsequent armistice which led to the occupation of half of France's territory. Pétain, a celebrated general, was appointed supreme leader of the unoccupied territory and endowed with significant authoritarian powers. Pétans control was premised on collaboration with German authorities. In this Speech Pétain outlines his vision for a renewed French nation. Candidates do not need any pre-existing knowledge of Petain or Vichy France and should not attempt to draw on outside knowledge.

Our domestic difficulties have sprung above all from troubled minds, from lack of men and from scarcity of products.

Troubled minds do not have as their sole origin the vicissitudes of our foreign policy. They come especially from our slowness in building a new order or, more correctly, in imposing one. The National Revolution has not yet taken its place among accomplished facts.[1]

It has not yet forced its way through because between the people and me--who understand one another so well--there has risen a double screen of partisans of the old regime and those serving the trusts.[2]

The troops of the old regime are legion. I rank among them without exception all who place their personal interests ahead of the permanent interests of the State--Freemasonry, political parties deprived of clientele but thirsting for a comeback, officials attached to an order of which they were beneficiaries and masters--or those who have subordinated the interests of the Fatherland to foreign interests.

A long wait will be needed to overcome the resistance of all these opponents of the new order, but we must start in now to smash their undertakings by decimating their leaders.

If France did not understand that she was condemned by the impact of events to change her regime, then she would see open up before her the abyss in which Spain of 1936 just missed being swallowed and from which she was saved only by faith, youth and sacrifice[3].

---

[1] 'National Revolution' was Pétains overarching framework for a project of national regeneration.
[2] The Old Regime is used as a byword for The Third Republic which ended with the armistice of 1940. Trust is deployed as a synonym for corporate interests
[3] Fascist dictator Franco had wrested power from a democratically elected Socialist government following a brutal civil war in 1936.

As for the power of the trusts, it is trying to reassert itself, using for its own ends the institution of Committees of Economic Organization. These committees were created, however, to rectify the errors of capitalism. They had in addition the purpose of entrusting responsible men with necessary authority to negotiate with Germany and assure equitable distribution of raw materials indispensable to our factories.

The choice of members for these committees was difficult. It was not always possible to find impartiality and competence united within the same minds. These provisional bodies created under the sway of a pressing need have been too numerous, too centralized and too unwieldy. The big corporations assumed too much authority and often inadmissible control.

In the light of experience, I shall correct the work I have undertaken, and I shall renew against a selfish and blind capitalism that struggle which the sovereigns of France waged and won against feudalism. I shall see to it that France is rid of the most despicable tutelage, that of money.

Irresponsible trade organizations, governed by commercial considerations, have too long been directing our food supply. I already have taken sanctions and struck at an entire system in the person of a single man; that of national distribution centers which have assured the great commercial agents exclusive and usurious control of all questions of food supply to the detriment of producer and consumer.

We are still suffering, but I do not wish our suffering displayed in front of the scandal of fortunes built out of the general misery. It would be all the more revolting, inasmuch as this nation has in the past year accomplished an immense labor, despite privations of all kinds and under the most difficult conditions.

I have in mind our farmers, who, without laborers, without fertilizer, without sulphate, have succeeded in obtaining results better than those of the year before. I have in mind the miners, who have worked without respite night and day to obtain coal for us. I have in mind all those workers who return from work only to find fireless homes and meagerly set tables.

It is thanks to their unceasing efforts that the life of the country has been able to be maintained, despite defeat. It is with them and through them that we will be able tomorrow to build a France free, powerful and prosperous. Let them wait with me for better times. The trials of France will have an end.

As for the lack of man power, that is due above all to the absence of those who are prisoners. As long as more than a million Frenchmen, comprising the young and vigorous elements of the nation and the best section of its elite, remain outside of the country's activities, it will be difficult to build a new and lasting edifice. Their return will make it possible to fill the great gap from which we suffer.[4] Their spirit, strengthened by camp life, matured by long reflection, will become the best cement of the National Revolution.

And yet, in spite of these difficulties the future of our country is being built with a precision that becomes more assured every day.

---

[4] Up to 2 million Frenchmen were held as POW's (Prisoners of War) in Germany following the armistice of 1940. Pétain attempted to implement a number of schemes to facilitate their return.

The family, communities, trades, provinces will be pillars of the constitution at which the best workers for our reconstruction are laboring tirelessly. Its preamble will open up clear perspectives for the future of France.

Our most recent reforms are being made the object of methodical revision, the outline of which will appear clearer as soon as legislative texts have been simplified and codified.

But lawmaking and building are not enough. Governing is needed. It is both the necessity and the will of the whole people.

This public opinion is today divided. France cannot be governed unless the initiative of her chief finds corresponding exactness and faithfulness in the bodies transmitting it. This exactness and faithfulness are still lacking.

France, however, cannot wait. A nation like ours, forged in the crucible of races and passions, proud and courageous, as ready for sacrifice as for violence and ever bristling when its honor is at stake, needs certainties, space and discipline.

What can you learn from this extract about the values of the author?

EXAMPLE ANSWERS

These answers were written under exam conditions by UniAdmissions tutors, none of whom have studied history at degree level but did study it at A level. This should mean that they represent an accurate picture of what a typical applicant's answer would look like, rather than a perfect answer written by a history PhD student.

They are each accompanied by examiner's comments, as well as a formal mark. These were marked by a former HAT marker at Oxford, so they should be an accurate representation of the kind of feedback and scoring that would occur in the real exam.

We recommend that you attempt each practice question yourself before turning to these answers, as practicing approaching the extract blind is among the most important parts of your preparation.

MOCK A ANSWER
What does this extract reveal about politics and society in Chiapas, Mexico in the 1990s?

It is clear from this passage that the Subcomondante is strongly motivated to highlight the injustice faced by the indigenous communities within the state of Chiapas. Throughout the passage, he refers to the efforts of the "powerful men" to only consider the indigenous communities as "touristic curiosities" and "anthropological objects". Both phrases remove all sense of humanity from the people themselves, possibly the root cause of the problems they face. As the rest of Mexico develops and integrates into modern globalised culture, the traditional ways of life of the Chiapanecos could be perceived as more rudimental to those in the cities throughout Mexico. The fact that the Subcomondante refers to the mispronunciation of both the name of the state and indigenous people by "the Mexiacans" tells us that their country no longer gives the original traditional communities the respect they hope for. With a growing disconnect and the fractures that develop from the duality between modern and traditional ways of life the existence of the indigenous communities not only in Chiapas, but throughout Mexico is threatened.

This is a substantial opening paragraph in which this candidate has opened with a clear statement of what they perceive to be the dominant theme of the passage as it relates to the question. It is important to remember that the HAT examiners want you to show your analytical skill, rather than a simple investigation of the source. In this example, it would be helpful if the candidate had clearly articulated what elements of politics and society they believe the Subcomandante is interacting with here. High-level indicators in the first paragraph include identifying the clear split between inhabitants of Mexico and 'Mexicans'. It would also be good if more could be made of the connection between 'powerful men' and 'the Mexicans'. Spelling mistakes like 'Mexiacans' and the constant misspelling of 'subcomandante' make it clear that this has been slightly rushed, but is a comparatively minor issue.

Through writing this letter, the Subcomondante seeks to appeal to "honest journalism" in order to convey accurate information regarding the indigenous communities. Previously in his letter, he refers to the presence of corruption at all levels, from "high-level federal functionaries to the last of the corrupt "Indigenous" leaders". With the problem being so widespread, it would be difficult to find media that could honestly portray the views the Subcomondate wishes to convey. At one point, he alludes to the fact that the Federal Army prevents such honesty being published, an act that emphasises the level of corruption being experienced at the present time. Furthermore, it seems as though dishonest journalism is being broadcast in order to reiterate the negative views that the government has of indigenous communities. The fact that the media is being so tightly controlled by Mexico's powerful men serves to highlight the political corruption occurring in Chiapas in the early 1990s.

There is a good point here; this is a society in which there is considerable interference in the press by the military and the well-defined Mexican establishment. Sadly, the point is a little hard to see in places. There is abundant evidence provided to support the claim that there is widespread corruption, but doesn't use that to make any clear statement about what impact this had on politics or society in Chiapas until the very end of the paragraph, at which point the HAT examiner could well have gotten lost. Remember to always try and make clear what point you are going to make at the top of your paragraphs before evidencing them. It's also interesting that the candidate refers to leaders, high-level functionaries, and powerful men, but still does not interact at all with whether these people are the entirety of 'the Mexicans'. Mexican identity is a significant component of the social structure of Chiapas at the time, and describing these two groups as the same without showing any awareness of why or how that is true has hurt them somewhat. This paragraph runs the risk of being a little too descriptive, without enough interaction about what the extract can really tell you about politics and society, for example that the political system encompasses political leaders for indigenous groups who are, in one way or another, unrepresentative of them, where the government is centralised, but which fails to provide basic needs for people 'in the mountains', and where power is devolved to local presidents who are equally unrepresentative, with an implication that elections are either unfair or not taking place.

The social structure of Chiapas appears to be based on wealth. Those with money have more of a say over how the state should be run. What this leads to is the large-scale suffering of the poorer communities as efforts to ensure they don't interfere with the development are undertaken. References to consumerism portray the wealthy as people motivated by material gains and globalisation, rather than focusing on the importance of national identity through the preservation of local traditions and ways of life. The growing divide appears to have upset society so much to the point that rebel groups decided to fight the federal enforcement in order to regain their identity. The passage shows how strong a cause this is for the people involved as the rebellion aren't frightened by the tanks, planes and helicopters, tools often associated with warfare, death and destruction. The core values of the rebel groups drive them to fight against larger powers and fight to retain their ways of life that were present before any of the modern concepts that are being rapidly introduced to both the state of Chiapas and Mexico itself.

This is a really promising paragraph, in which the candidate has carried out real source analysis. The coverage of social and financial inequality is good, and the paragraph opens with a direct focus on society, which makes it much easier to satisfy the examiner's requirements. There is mention of consumerism and a culture focused on the accumulation of wealth and ornament, but more evidence could be brought in here (such as Marcos's mention of "ornamental works" "imported products" and NAFTA). Mentioning globalisation is good, though it would be really good to see a brief discussion of how Marcos clearly identified NAFTA as a further step in the wrong direction, and was presumably a significant political factor. The paragraph from "The passage shows" onwards doesn't have a clear point relating to politics or society, although there is one in there, and this could be more clearly expressed.

As this extract was written in 1994, the problems of corruption, propaganda and the gradual eradication of traditional ways of life can be assumed to have been occurring years prior to the publication of this letter. If it was eventually picked up and distributed by the local and national press, I would like to think the importance of fair representation of the indigenous communities within the state of Chiapas improved. But the issues of corruption and media control could potentially have prevented this and therefore limited any positive change in the remainder of the decade.

It is good that the candidate has taken time to explore the nature of the source, and what they can learn from it, this should have been done at the top of the essay. There are missed opportunities here to make fundamental points which, while obvious, have not been stated by the candidate and certainly will not be assumed by the examiner. Things like the fact that there is a military insurgency taking place in Chiapas, and that the society there supports an armed insurgency which has previously been repressed and targeted by the state army, and that the EZLN was one of a number of anti-government groups actively participating in warfare, with the intent of creating meaningful political change whereby the state government is altered or replaced. What is good is that the candidate has identified that there could be a gap between this letter being written, and being published, and we don't know whether it was actually ever released to the public at all. Attention on the extent to which this letter could generate change is superfluous, and not part of the question. Your knowledge here extends to January 1994 and no further. A minor technical point is that the candidate should have avoided use of the first person in their final paragraph, for the sake of consistency if nothing else. It would also have been useful to collect the other information that the candidate had been able to learn about society and politics, but not analysed in full, could be mentioned in a brief paragraph before the last one.

Points to consider which weren't mentioned include: the ELZN seeking to contact people outside of Mexico, the separation of 'the public' from 'the Mexicans', that the army is comprised exclusively of men, that warfare is seen as a political matter and a political solution will end the military conflict. Other points include native society is marred by injustices and that the death of indigenous people has not troubled the central government until they began to engage in warfare, that NAFTA was intended in some way to 'disappear' indigenous populations, that the 'corrupt "indigenous" leaders were decreasing in numbers in some way (perhaps as a result of warfare?), that "the Mexicans" arrived in Mexico a long time after the indigenous population, and that one of the most important social values is dignity, which had been denied the people of Chiapas. We also know that there is poor education in Chiapas, and that the rebellion is based upon secret groups.

Overall the answer contains some good analysis, but hasn't been checked prior to submission and which seems quite thin on direct responses to the question. It does have some high-level indicators, as mentioned above, but overall this would be a tier-two answer, with a final mark of around 25/40.

MOCK B ANSWER
What does this extract reveal about the nature of early anti-colonial nationalism in India?

To begin with, as the extract is a primary source, we can assume a moderate amount of validity in its interpretation of the Indian political climate. Mohandas K Gandhi is said to be a prominent figure in the Indian nationalist movement, meaning his writings are likely to be accurate and in accordance with the political discourses of the time. From this one can conclude that it is generally to be trusted regarding its commentary on the nature of early anti-colonial nationalism.

This is a brief opening which addresses important points of origin for the source. It is good to highlight strengths, but you should always do so alongside limitations, which are certainly extant. An important observation that the candidate has made here is that Gandhi is said to be a prominent figure, making his testimony more broadly representative of early anti-colonial nationalism. Many candidates fall into the trap of bringing in outside knowledge when dealing with particularly famous figures like Gandhi, and it's important not to do so. This paragraph does a good job of setting up the source, but it would be nice to get a hint at the main theme(s) that they had identified about colonialism within the first paragraph. Examiners don't want to have to wait until the second one to have an idea of what this is actually going to say. The easiest solution would be to combine the two.

Early anti-colonial nationalism in India is depicted by this extract as very much in its infancy: the dialogue illustrates that there is much contention over the most effective manifestation of Hind Swaraj, and that the very question of whether India should self-determine is yet to be answered convincingly. Evidence for this can be found frequently in the text.

This is a great observation, well communicated. You've got one point, that nationalism is ill-defined and nascent, with evidence to support it, and it is articulated in a way which uses the language of the question to clearly demonstrate relevance. The bulk of the real supporting evidence for this is in the next paragraph though, which is a slightly odd division. These could be combined.

First, quotations such as "You may think so; I do not" and "This is not the Swaraj that I want" are clear indications that the dialogue represents a lack of agreement over the nature of Swaraj. The Reader is shown to be more idealistic in his interpretation, referring to the thought of political philosophers such as Spencer and Mill in explaining his vision, while the Editor is far more sceptical of these claims, arguably adopting a pragmatic position. This indicates that the early anti-colonial nationalist movement in India is yet to adopt a clear stance regarding its self-determination.

This runs the risk of repeating the points made in the previous paragraph, it would read much better if this paragraph (excluding the last sentence) was combined with the previous one. What is really good to see though is consistent returning to the question itself, and making sure that there is a clear answer being provided throughout. The candidate has also shown that they have considered the implications of this split. While there is a lot here on the fact that there is debate, surprisingly little has been made of what the substance of that debate comprised.

Second, the very nature of the extract shows that early anti-colonial nationalism in India is in a certain state of turmoil. Gandhi intentionally chooses the format of a dialogue in order to represent the many viewpoints expressed by people discussing early anti-colonial nationalism. The fact that this pamphlet contains a discourse rather than a manifesto indicates that the floor is very much open for debate regarding what form Indian nationalism should take.

At this point, an awful lot has been made of the fact that early nationalism is in turmoil, with little else by way of analysis. It is good that they discuss the fact that the passage itself exists in the form of a written debate with a single author, but this point should have been made as part of a single paragraph on the point concerning nationalism as undefined, alongside others. Other points they could make to flesh this out include the 'awakening' of nationalism caused by Partition, and lead by the INC. They could also have talked about the fact that this early nationalism was marked by discontent and unrest, and that this is something that people have wanted from some time (based on the formation date for the INC and Ghandi's mention of impatience. Another point may be the fact that, for some, independence is built on removing English control, while for others it is about dismantling the institutions which the English installed, and transforming India's political and social makeup. A point could also be made about national identity, and that the English and Indians were both assumed to have an immutable national identity, what Indian identity meant was only hard to agree on because of the presence of the English.

The purpose of the source is likely informative, as it is a pamphlet written by Gandhi in a native Indian language. In the early twentieth century pamphlets were an effective means to convey information to a large number of people, and the fact that it is written in Gujarati rather than English means its target audience is the Indian people. However, as previously discussed by this essay, it expresses not a single viewpoint but a debate. Gandhi's intent is not to sway the Indian people to one specific side but rather present them with the arguments of multiple aspects of Indian nationalism. Again, this reinforces the point that there is yet to be a majority opinion on the precise form of Hind Swaraj, and that as a whole, early anti-colonial nationalism in India lacked a definitive approach to the issue of colonial rule. Furthermore one could consider its analysis of the political climate to be fairly objective, in that Gandhi's own opinion is not prominently placed but involved in the discourse like any other viewpoint.

There is a lot of information condensed into this source, and not all of it comes from the paper. Interaction with the way pamphlets were used in the 20th century, for example, is not something that can be determined from the source (and the candidate has certainly made no effort to do so). Bringing in this information is a low-level indicator for the candidate and harms their final mark considerably. The other main point the candidate makes in this paragraph is that Gandhi used the format of a dialogue, and that this shows that early-anti-colonial nationalism lacked a definitive approach. This is the same point made in the previous paragraph, and realistically this entire paragraph could be cut for a net positive.

A point can also be made regarding the anti-colonial, or potentially pro-colonial, aspect of nationalism in India. In the extract the Reader presents the view that "we should copy the English people" in the Indian approach to nationalism, with the argument that it will allow them to resist future colonisation or external influence. However, the Editor argues that in doing so "you would make India English": India would be so similar to England that life under a nationalist regime would be identical to British colonisation, defeating the purpose of Hind Swaraj and self-government. For this reason, it could be argued that the extract shows some exponents of Indian nationalism to not be anti-colonial at all. If the English political structure and tradition is kept, then surely driving away the English is for nothing? Gandhi urges his readers to consider this point, leaving one to conclude that while one may support Indian nationalism, its manifestation as an English proxy state with homogenous culture is very much a potential outcome.

Here, the candidate has shown us a bit more insight into the specific divide in interpretations of nationalism hinted at previously, which is good. There is more evidence that they should have brought in to support their claim about the Reader wanting an English approach to nationalism, for example the point Ghandi makes as the reader about the English Parliament being the Mother of Parliaments. There is a danger in this paragraph that the candidate strays too much into description, without any serious interaction with the issue of what these conflicting views can tell us. For example, you could use the observations the candidate has made here to say that it shows that a core component of the nationalist debate was conflicting notions of Indian national identity, and therefore that re-establishing and Indian national identity was needed, and early anti-colonial nationalism in India had formed, in part, due to the erasure of Indian national identity brought about by the constant deprivation of Indian wealth, agency, and freedom by the British Empire.

In conclusion, the extract shows us that the nature of early anti-colonial nationalism in India is in controversy for its supporters. The movement is still in its fledgling form as there is clear contention over many aspects, such as the manifestation of Hind Swaraj and the eviction of the British.

The meaning here is not entirely clear. Is the candidate arguing that there is current debate on the nature of Indian nationalism, or a complex historiography, or that there was a controversial element of the nationalist movement for pro-nationalists in India? The only real point made seems to be that the movement was nascent, this is a good point, but it cannot stand on its own, and further conclusions could be drawn, in addition to the ones mentioned above, from the existence of the pamphlet itself.

Overall, this response is deficient in a few areas. There is a good point made about the amorphous, developing nature of the anti-colonial national movement. There is little nuance to the point, which is restated several times without the candidate taking their conclusions any further to comment on the state of national sentiment, nationalist movements, or anti-colonialism in India at the time. The response also integrates some of the candidate's own knowledge, and while there is good attention paid to responding to the question, the structure could use some work. Overall, this answer falls some way short of the average mark for successful applicants (28/40), securing 22 marks in total.

MOCK C ANSWER

What does this extract tell us about the author's opinions on religion and religious practices?

1.   Sophisticated religion is that which is not materialistic, but worships a higher being
2.   Superstitious religions died out in his utopia as they were disproven by sophisticated religion
3.   ?
4.   Religion can be unique to the individual and they may debate amongst themselves but bitterness and resentment will only lead to violence and slavery
5.   Everyone should be religious in some way as those who are not and who attribute the complexities of the world to chance will ultimately break laws and be a detriment to society

HAT examiners never mark your essay plans, but if you put them in the answer booklet they will see them, and if they do it can help them (entirely subconsciously) follow your argument a little better sometimes.

Thomas More used his fictional work of Utopia to express his idealistic opinions towards religion. His attitudes are reflective of the benefits and problems with religion in society, so it is interesting to place his solutions to such issues in a utopian context. One stance towards religion that he expresses in the first two paragraphs of this extract is what he believes to be the wisest and greatest form of religion. He talks of some Utopans to be worshiping "the sun, others the moon or one of the planets. Some worship such men as have been eminent in former times for virtue or glory". He goes on to say that the greater worship is actually that of an "incomprehensible Deity", describing an omnipotent Being who created and controls everything. This juxtaposition is reflective of real-world examples: with ancient Greek and Roman religions from antiquity being easily comparable to the Utopan religions that worship the sun, moon, planets or important figures from the past. The omnipotent deism that More described as the greater religion, that eventually goes on to out-live the superstitious types of religion, draws parallels with Christiantiy. By dubbing this as the superior, more sophisticated religion, More is expressing his opinion that religions without superstitions that can be easily disproved are superior and are more timeless, and this is why they survive longer on his Utopia.

The candidate has done a good job to mention and immediately dismiss the fact that the source is fiction. That has no bearing on the value of the source to your investigation, and should be acknowledged and nothing more. The candidate makes a good point, that More sees religion as diverse, but those which cannot be easily disprove last the longest. This is a very unusual HAT question, focusing on the opinions of the author, rather than the values of their time, and this means that there is a limited scope for using the author's values to make extrapolations about the range of religions in existence at the time, but this candidate has done a good job of demonstrating More's opinion on religion. As the opening paragraph, improvements could be made with a clear summary of the main points covered in the essay, as well as something on the limitations of the source and how they are to be counteracted. Repeated misspelling of "Utopian" and "Christianity" doesn't look good.

Another way in which he expresses his ambivalence towards religion is through the benefits that religion can have on individuals, and therefore how this can benefit society. In the final paragraph of this extract, More says that, while it may not matter exactly what religion is practised, there is a distinct law in Utopia that insists the recognition of the greatness of the world and therefore the belief of a higher power. He emphasises that men who only fear the laws that society binds them by will do whatever they can to break those laws, since they don't believe in a greater punishment that can be inflicted by a higher power. This would be problematic for society as it would cause unrest, thus explaining why a law enforcing some form of spiritual belief would be necessary in Utopia. However, he does also state that a man cannot be forced to believe something he simply does not, so the law would be enforced in the way of education. This ideology reflects More's potential disdain for the forced and restrictive power that religion had within real society. In an ideal world, More believed that religion should be used by individuals to unite them and grant them with self-happiness and motivation to contribute to society, and that this was the most useful purpose of religion in society.

The candidate introduces this paragraph with a link to More's ambivalence towards religion, even though that isn't a point the candidate has previously made. This is evidence of a poorly arranged argument, or poor communication, both of which are low-level indicators. There is a good point in there about the fact that More sees religion as a stabilising influence, which limits people's desire to behave recklessly, but it is not made strongly, or directly connected to the question. Furthermore, the candidate uses this point to talk about More's disdain for the role of religion within his society, though this is not evidenced, and the question does not ask for information about the society More lives in. This means that the candidate's point is only about More's disdain for religions, which needs to be thoroughly evidenced in order for it to make sense within the context of this passage.

Leading on from this, it is apparent from the penultimate paragraph that More was not blind to the potential pitfalls that can befall religion in society and besmirch its reputation. He made a law in Utopia stating that anyone could follow whatever religion they pleased and was allowed to preach that belief system, so long as the debate between religious practices was done in amicable ways. In Utopia, this was following quarrels of the previous inhabitants that surrounded differing religious practices. This had actually weakened the power that religion should have in society, and instead of uniting people, it disbanded them. More could see the potential that violence over religion could have towards contributing to violence and slavery, which is why he imposed a law against such open resentment towards other religions in his Utopia. This therefore reflects More's angst against the tension between different religions in the real world and his understanding behind the disadvantages that religion can have.

The candidate takes quite a while to get to their point, clear communication is really important in your response to the HAT question (especially so when you have such a complex passage to analyse). The point here is, on its own, a good one, that More sees religion as something which is damaging when there is too much disagreement, or in other words that religion is at its most beneficial when it is shared by all. More in fact alludes to the fact that Utopia was conquered in no small part because its inhabitants could not agree on religious issues, the inclusion of this history of the fictional place makes it clear that this is a deliberate example being made for the express purpose of showing religion's shortcomings. It would be good if more evidence was provided to support the candidate's claims, and less time was spent describing what More had said. The examiners will know what the passage says very well, what they are interested in is your ability to recognise the truths present within them. More believed religious freedom to be important, he believed that religious discourse should be managed and civil, and that without such civility it could create ruin, etc. These points should be evidenced, and clearly stated so that the examiner knows just what you are saying More's opinion on religion and religious practice are.

To conclude, this extract from Thomas More's Utopia sheds light on More's positive attitude towards religion. He believed in deism and was against superstition, and he thought that deism would always outlast superstitious religious practices in society. He also thought religion to be necessary in order to maintain order in society. However, More did believe that there were necessary changes to be made in order for religion to prosper in society as he believed it rightfully should.

This conclusion is something HAT examiners see all the time, and is a real shame. The conclusion does not follow from the essay. The candidate first argues that More is idealistic towards religion, then that his is ambivalent, and then that it can be a destabilising influence. That does not add up to a positive attitude towards religion. It is true that More was a Deist, and not a fan of idolatry, but there is considerable room here for more substantive statements about More's opinion on whether Religion should be managed by laws, on the relationship between faith and religion (in the part about the unordained priest), and for anything on religious practice, which is half of the question (based on the unpacking methods covered in this guide) and yet hasn't been explicitly examined at all.

The candidate has tried to bring together a range of conflicting views into a single narrative, which was made more difficult by a highly complex source and an unusual style of question. High level indicators include recognising that a work of fiction can tell you a lot about the author's opinions by virtue of recognising that they chose to include everything written there, as well as talking about the fact that More saw religion as something which should be governed by law. Other ones which were missed include talking about the fact that Utopia is idealised, and therefore the state of religion More describes there is what he wants the most, and points about the importance of practicing religion to true devotion. Overall, this paper secured 23/40.

MOCK D ANSWER
What does this extract reveal about society in 14th century Florence?

Through the reaction of individuals during the plague that occurred during the 14th Century in Italy, the author reveals key dichotomies and opposing ideas through epitomising them within the behavior of different groups of society. Such oppositions more broadly refer to the contrast between religion and scientific observation, the choices of the individual and societies and how one's own behavior influences others. In doing so, the author presents a mixed and conflicted view of society during this troubled and challenging time.

The candidate has done a good job here identifying that it's through the reported behaviours that we can see elements of society. It would also be good to include the observation here that the author's commentary on these behaviours is also an important component, and the author themselves provide crucial insight into 14th century Florentine society. Their second sentence is part of a good HAT introduction, short and summarising some of the main ways in which society can be demonstrated. What this is missing is a clear answer to the question. What does this opposition, and this conflicted view, mean for what it reveals to you, the candidate, about 14th century Florentine society?

Paragraph 2:

In reference to causes of the plague, the author routinely refers to religiosity, in doing so marking the overarching importance of belief during these times and it's power in influencing not only the views of individuals but society as a whole.

Here, the candidate has identified one of the components of society, religion.

This is exemplified by how the author describes the occurrence of the plague as a "wrath of God" due to the "operation of heavenly bodies", caused by the lack of morality within society.

Here they've been able to connect their evidence to additional detail about Florentine society, that some equated religiosity with morality and that a more pious society would be a more moral one.

This suggests that society exclusively believed such events were both caused by God and brought upon the world due to its failings as a form of punishment.

I think here, the conclusion almost makes sense, though the candidate has made a mistake by saying society exclusively believed such events. There is no proof of exclusivity, and indeed the author's description of ones who are devout, or worthy of belief, implies equally the existence of others?

This is further emphasised in the second paragraph when the author highlights the helplessness of physicians yet in doing so, once more refers to the immorality within Italian society through the actions of individuals "who had never had any teaching of medicine".

Here, the candidate is making an interesting point, but it is hard to understand. Clarity of expression is always very important in the HAT, as the examiners can't give you the benefit of the doubt. It's also unclear why the helplessness of physicians equates to this being a divine punishment, the candidate could have cured this by more clearly spelling out that medical intervention actually accelerated the disease and that was used to imply punishment for attempting to interfere with the plague which was "sent down upon mankind for our correction by the just wrath of God"

Although primarily a piece of descriptive writing peppered with rhetorical questions, it seems that the writer himself is subtly aligning his views with the notions of inflicted punishment due to the immorality of society through such observations.

I think that the candidate has missed a trick here. The author isn't just aligning his views with existing notions of punishment, the author is layering themselves into everything they write (this is pretty common for eyewitness accounts). The author's decisions about what was and was not important, and what constituted a divine punishment, or virtue, are all really valuable indicators for social values at the time, as you know that Bocaccio was a prominent writer.

Paragraph 3:
The passage also includes a somewhat conflicting idea to such simple causality through its inclusion of long descriptions of symptoms and the authors own observations, in itself a hypocritical act when compared to the authors scorning the ignorance of "non medical practitioners".

This is an interesting point, but the logic needs to be more clearly demonstrated. Just as in GCSE maths you have to always show your working to get full marks, you need to show your thinking in the HAT. How does medical observation conflict with causality? Why does a description of the symptoms of the disease equate to attempted medical practice? The quotation provided is not a direct reference to the material either.

Descriptions of the plagues "dolorous effects" suggest a shift in mentality within Italian society at the time, from religious explanations to a form of inquiry and understanding.

This is a good point, and I think it is valid, but the candidate hasn't brought in the best evidence for this. They would be better served by focusing on the author's descriptions of transmission via material, the various manifestations of plague boils, and the understanding that isolation limits the risk of contracting the disease – the latter in particular could be argued to be an indicator that the disease was not solely understood to be the wrath of god. This could be helped by more detailed note taking during their reading and review stages!

An example of this, although not in the author's own words, is the aim to explain the transmission of the disease through the consideration of its spread not only between human beings but also "animals foreign to the human species". In doing so, the author describes both his own and others scepticism and astonishment following the transmission of the disease from pieces of clothing to "two hogs".

This is a good example of the fact that the author was clearly observing the population. However, that doesn't really make any point about society on its own, a shift to a form of inquiry is a little thin. The points you could make here are that this was a society in which people were known to tell falsehoods, and that writing things down was only considered valuable if you knew them to be true.

It is here once more that the conflict and inner dialogue of the author and indeed society between that which they believe and the act of intrinsic human act of inquiry. In this, the author is perhaps underlining a key shift occurring in Italian society as new advancements in science occur that may conflict previously held beliefs.

While it is good that the candidate has made an effort to return to the shores of relevance, this seems an almighty stretch. Connecting observations of animal behaviour and epidemiology to a shift in Florentine society to a broader adoption of science is tricky based on this source alone, and this might hint that the candidate is bringing in their own knowledge. The first sentence, incidentally, makes little sense.

Paragraph 4:

The author also refers to the different reactions of individuals to the plague within the final paragraph where two different mentalities are described. The first involves individuals isolating and living "removed from every other" while the second contrasts this through the act to "carouse (...) and go about singing". In this, the author contacts the notions of the individual and wider society and the dichotomy this poses in the influence and effects of one's own behavior not only on themselves but on society as a whole.

I think there could be something interesting in here, but the candidate has done such a poor job of communicating their idea that it wouldn't be worth any marks. In Florentine society people behaved differently, but what does this really tell us. Points could be made here about the fact that there existed a group of society which enjoyed drinking and partying, and this was not seen as immoral or sinful, but was certainly no better than the apparent virtue in keeping 'oneself from all excess' – you could really expand on that to talk about attitudes to consumption, especially considering what you know about the source, that it is the tale of ten people who pursue this path, and isolate themselves.

This shows an inner dialogue for the author themselves where the reaction of certain groups within society is in itself a "very barbarous conclusion" that led to the plague and now is simply exemplified through such reactions.

The barbarous conclusion in question was turning their back on others and isolating themselves, the subject of the book. What does this tell you about society, as the author saw it, that people should help each other. If barbarity is the antithesis of society, then society should be about existing together in cooperation, based on this description and value judgment.

Therefore, the passage tackles the issues within Italian society indirectly on numerous levels, including both the authors own beliefs and inner conflicts, whilst also considering themes such as religion, medicine, scientific observation and morality in addition to the presentation of current events as metaphors to present wider ideas. In doing so, the author utilizes the plague as an apt example to show key differences within society that result from shifts in beliefs and behaviors and which highlight the immoral behaviours of certain groups that were perhaps the cause of the plague itself.

The conclusion does a good job of summarising many of the candidates own points, the main weakness is those points themselves. Good source analysis and planning skills will help make sure you don't make the same mistakes. This example secured a total of 17/40.

MOCK E ANSWER
What does this extract tell us about gender and sexual practices in late fourteenth century England?

Within this extract, the court case of John Ryneker can be analysed to reveal attitudes towards gender and sexual practices in later fourteenth century England.

The examiners know this, if they didn't, they would not have been able to set this question! You don't need to make statements like this.

During this late fourteenth century, this extract suggests that women carrying out sex work were not uncommon.

Okay, so we have one clear point here, which is good.

John Britby's testimonial describes him requesting Rykener's services 'asking him as he would a woman if he could commit a libidinous act with her'. This highlights the commonplace of this service. Rykener also references 'a certain Anna' as also being a sex worker which strengthens this argument.

They've done a good job of evidencing this point.

Moreover, throughout the testimony, Rykener refers to having sex with several men 'with him as with a woman' which further supports this.

I think at this stage there risks being an excess of supporting evidence for what is, fundamentally, a fairly minor individual claim. There is, however, a really interesting point to be made here on gender identity which hasn't quite come up.

Despite this, it may not have been common for men to be sex workers as Rykener 'confessed' that he had sex with a 'certain Joan'. Confession also suggests that this was also a considered wrongdoing.

I think this is a fair assumption to make, based on the text, but it would be really good to tie this in more directly to the question. It tells us that sex work was a component of sexuality, and women usually offered it while men usually paid for it. We also know that sex workers were involved in the education and care of other sex workers, and would also teach particular ideas, acts, or behaviours to people through or alongside their work. If this additional point had been made, this would have shown the high level thinking needed for a good answer!

However, although sex work may have been common, the act of sodomy is referred to in a very negative way throughout the extract, describing it as 'detestable unmentionable and ignominous vice' and as 'detestable wrongdoings'.

Okay, so we have another point here about a specific sexual behaviour, with a range of evidence to support it, which is good.

This demonstrates that sodomical sexual practices were condemned.

I'm not sure 'sodomical' is a word, it might be better to simply say that this was a society in which certain types of sex were acceptable, where others are not.

Despite this, the account of Rykener details that he had sex with over fifteen men.

Perhaps considerably more. It may be indelicate but it could be worth pointing out that all of these instances of sex with men would have constituted a kind of sex which was unacceptable.

This suggests that sodomy was indeed practiced. Perhaps, due to the condemnation of the act, men such as Rykener dressing up as a woman enabled men who wished to have sex with another man to be able to do this covertly.

This is a really interesting inference about sexuality and gender, which could go a long way, but it needs to be its own paragraph really – there are questions about the extent to which these men were deceived (or merely maintained the pretense of deception) and conclusions can be drawn from that about gay sex and gender roles. In this case, the point is good, but without the explanation or evidence to back it up it can't qualify as a high-level indicator.

This is supported by Rykener practicing this act with Sir Walter 'often'.

I think the candidate is trying to imply here that Sir Walter would, presumably, not have had illusions about Rykener's anatomy. This isn't particularly clear though, and so could have been stated much more clearly as a claim that men who wanted to have sex with men may well have often done so by having one of them dress as a woman (though it is unclear whether that was the case in this example).

In terms of gender, this extract suggests that women were seen as temptresses, as Rykener acted under the guise of 'Eleanor' while men were more innocent and naive to their ploys.

This next and final point, is a very simple one about gender roles. There is little information provided in the source about gender roles specifically, and this lacks the level of analysis and thinking required by HAT examiners. They will, instead, be wanting candidates to talk about what the repeated comments about women's clothing, having sex 'as a woman' and being approached 'as a woman' can tell us about gender identity. While in women's clothing, was Rykener John, or Eleanor? Gender identity appears to be, in Rykener's case, fluid, and asking questions about what this means for gender in fourteenth century England would be really valuable.

For example, men in the extract have been described as 'three unsuspecting scholars'. Yet, one of them practiced sexual acts with Rykener often. This demonstrates the blame being put on the 'woman' - in this case Rykener.

This is a really important point, from an objective standpoint both people involved in the sexual encounter are 'men' in the eyes of the law – blame is put on the person presenting as female, even if they aren't (as it is clear from the opening paragraph that the court did not recognise Rykener's gender as being anything other than male). The focus here is on othering, on targeting those who do not conform, and both sexuality and gender were clearly battlefields for enforcing conformity in an environment in which many did not conform!

This echoes 'original sin' biblically, where Eve tempts Adam away from the path of goodness.

Own knowledge, very bad idea, don't include it as it will lower your mark.

Similarly, this is how Rykener is described, as he takes on the role of Eleanor, tricking men to commit this act.

The issue of whether Rykener is taking on a role as Eleanor, or whether they actually identify as Eleanor has not been addressed, but needs to be.

As well as this, there is a clear attitude of male superiority and power in this era, highlighted by the roles men could take - from Alderman to scholars, while women appear to have much smaller roles, such as embroidesses.

This is a good piece of observation.

In conclusion, this extract demonstrates the common role of women as sex workers, echoes male superiority and shuns sodomy, which may have been covertly practiced.

Overall, this is a poor answer. First and foremost, it is alarmingly short. HAT answers don't need to be long, but there is a real lack of detail here which could be remedied just by writing more. There are also serious issues with the candidate missing significant points about gender and sex, as mentioned above, and carrying out detailed analysis. This could be remedied through careful reading and unpacking the question more thoroughly. The final mark was 14/40.

As an additional note: the original version of this response contained a range of different terms for sex workers and people who had sex, some of which were either slurs or clear value judgments on the part of the student. Value judgments are always low-level indicators, more importantly; historians should, in general, refrain from using prejudices and judgments of today to shape our interpretation of the past, and you should try to refrain from allowing personal prejudices about particular demographics or occupations from entering your work.

FINAL ADVICE

Arrive well rested, well fed and well hydrated

The HAT is an intense test, so make sure you're ready for it. Ensure you get a good night's sleep before the exam (there is no point cramming) and don't miss breakfast. If you're taking water into the exam then make sure you've been to the toilet before so you don't have to leave during the exam.

Make Notes on your Essay

You may get asked questions on your essay at the interview. Given that there is sometimes more than four weeks from the HAT to the interview, it is really important to make short notes on the essay title and your main arguments after the essay. You'll thank yourself after the interview if you do this.

Afterword

Remember that the route to a high score is your approach and practice. Don't fall into the trap that "*you can't prepare for the HAT*"– this could not be further from the truth. With knowledge of the test, some useful time-saving techniques and plenty of practice you can dramatically boost your score.

Work hard, never give up and do yourself justice.

Good luck!

Acknowledgements

I would like to express my sincerest thanks to the many people who helped make this book possible, not least of which my wife Chloe, and the Oxford Tutors who shared their expertise in compiling these questions and answers.

Toby

About Us

UniAdmissions publish over 100 titles across a range of subject areas, covering specialised admissions tests, examination techniques, personal statement guides, plus everything else you need to improve your chances of getting on to competitive courses such as medicine and law, as well as into universities such as Oxford and Cambridge.

Outside of publishing we also operate a highly successful tuition division. This company was founded in 2013 by Dr Rohan Agarwal and Dr David Salt, both Cambridge Medical graduates with several years of tutoring experience. Since then, every year hundreds of applicants and schools work with us on our programmes. Through the programmes we offer, we deliver expert tuition, exclusive course places, online courses, best-selling textbooks and much more.

With a team of over 1,000 Oxbridge tutors and a proven track record, UniAdmissions has quickly become the UK's number one admissions company.

Visit and engage with us at:
Website (UniAdmissions): www.uniadmissions.co.uk
Facebook: www.facebook.com/uniadmissionsuk
Twitter:

Your Free Book

Thanks for purchasing this Ultimate Book. Readers like you have the power to make or break a book –hopefully you found this one useful and informative. *UniAdmissions* would love to hear about your experiences with this book. As thanks for your time we'll send you another ebook from our Ultimate Guide series absolutely <u>FREE</u>!

How to Redeem Your Free Ebook

1) Find the book you have on your Amazon purchase history or your email receipt to help find the book on Amazon.

2) On the product page at the Customer Reviews area, click 'Write a customer review'. Write your review and post it! Copy the review page or take a screen shot of the review you have left.

3) Head over to www.uniadmissions.co.uk/free-book and select your chosen free ebook!

Your ebook will then be emailed to you – it's as simple as that!

You can buy all of our titles in print and electronically through Amazon.co.uk

Printed in Great Britain
by Amazon

699a693b-dc87-4ec7-9b63-b0ff62a1ff1fR01